The Dandelion

The Dandelion

Terry Guilford

Cover design by: Kahren Richardson

Balboa Press books may be ordered through booksellers or by contacting:

Balboa Press
A Division of Hay House
1663 Liberty Drive
Bloomington, IN 47403
www.balboapress.com
1 (877) 407-4847

Print information available on the last page.

ISBN: 978-1-4525-2118-3 (sc)
ISBN: 978-1-4525-2119-0 (e)

Balboa Press rev. date: 05/10/2019

Contents

Ten percent of the proceeds from this book are donated to World Vision for their work with children around the world.

For Clare, the best daughter a mother could have

...

Many, many thanks to Jerry and Esther Hicks

Chapter 1

The Deep, Dark Well

"My dearest, darling Michael,

I am leaving you and you know why. I love you and I am leaving you today.

It feels so good to be able to say that, so exhilarating and so powerful. *I* am leaving you. I feel like jumping up and down and punching the air and screaming, yes, I am doing it! I am *leaving* you. After 30 years together and two beautiful children, I am going. There is no longer any reason for me to stay. I waited ten long, painful months for you to leave *me* until I couldn't stand the powerless, helpless feeling anymore. Now I am leaving *you.* I am leaving you *today,* December 12.

I haven't always felt this good. Ten months ago, I felt isolated and paralyzed with fear. I don't feel that way now, but rather the reverse. I feel outrageously happy and excited. I feel fabulous.

In two minutes, I will phone you at your office to make sure you are back from Perth. I will ask you to open the email and attachment from me as soon as you are free. I will hang up and then I will press send. Please read the attachment, my letter to you, Mike. It will help you understand what I have just done to you.

In half an hour you will receive by courier a small envelope with a post office box key and a storage unit key in it. You will need to sign for it.

Then you will understand.

Why didn't you tell me? I imagine you asking. I am telling you now, I reply. Please read this. *Why have you written to me?* I hear you ask. I have written you this letter because I just had to write it. I want and need to explain. For thirty years, you were my lover, husband and best friend. You were the person I could tell anything and everything to. When I had an interesting day, I always thought, I must tell my dearest darling – my Mike. I still do, because habits can be hard to break. I still want to tell you everything that is interesting or important to me, but I intend to let that fade with time.

For now, I am writing to tell you what has happened to me over the past ten months before your unseeing eyes, condensed from some recordings with my therapist and the journal she encouraged me to write. *You've been seeing a therapist? Since when?* I hear you ask. Yes, I have. Seeing a therapist is one of the many things I have been doing over the past ten months to help me come to this decision.

Why didn't you just tell me, or deliver this letter yourself? I hear you ask. I couldn't give it to you in person, my darling, because I'm a coward. I don't want to see you. I am afraid that if I see your beloved face, I might change my mind. The last time I saw you, four days ago, you hugged me, picked up your suitcase, smiled and kissed me goodbye. That was the last and best image I have of you and I don't want to spoil it. I might have had some satisfaction from seeing the expression on your face today if I spoke to you or gave you a letter, but I simply couldn't risk it and it wouldn't be worth it.

Believe me, I thought about it. I thought about it a lot. Over the past month, I have imagined a variety of scenarios. You might be shocked, horrified and disbelieving. You might cry. You might beg me to stay, which would be very satisfying. You might be relieved, delighted or even euphoric, which would not. Either way, I don't want to remember you that way. I want my last image of you to be one in which you smile and kiss me goodbye.

Why did you send the keys to my office? I hear you ask. I needed to be sure you would receive them. That woman works in your office and the envelope may have become 'mislaid' so I am making sure you receive it by arranging for you to sign for it. Besides, the office is the only place I can send it – don't ask. Just read the letter. By doing it this way, I can leave you – no discussion, no negotiation, no drama - just a done deal.

I have also written this letter because I believe there will be tough times ahead for you, sweetheart, and the strategies I learned from my therapist may help you the way they helped me.

I have loved you since I was eighteen years old. I still love you and I am forty-eight. You are, and probably always will be, the love of my life, and I am finally at a place where I can honestly say that I want you to be happy, simply because if you are happy, maybe you will leave me alone to be happy too.

I want you to know how I went from holding my breath every time you walked through the door, to breathing freely and easily, no matter where you were or what you were doing. I want you to know how I went from having my happiness depend on your every move, to discovering that my happiness depends entirely on my ability to focus on who I am and what *I* want.

How did you find out? I hear you ask. I saw you with another woman on Wednesday, February 8 – the day my life fell apart. It was two o'clock in the afternoon, two months after my Mum died, six days after our twenty-sixth wedding anniversary and three days after we had to have lovely old Molly put down.

I had been over to your parents' house, just as I did every Wednesday morning, to check their medications and order their groceries.

I was cycling across the park to meet four of my friends for coffee at the Pavilion Café when I saw the two of you together in the Fitzroy Gardens. You were sitting under a tree about thirty meters away on a rug with a young, blonde woman. You were kissing her, holding her hands, smiling and talking. The two of you were totally engrossed in each other. I was watching lovers who knew each other well. I got off my bike for another look. It was definitely you; there was no doubt about it. To make sure,

I phoned you. I saw you take out your phone, look at the screen for a second, touch it and toss it aside. The phone went dead at my end. You knew it was me and you tossed me aside. I stood still. I couldn't move. I couldn't breathe. The betrayal I felt was overwhelming. Then, something unexpected happened. I started to tremble and wet my pants. And not just a little; I lost the lot. My bladder simply let go.

Warm urine ran down the inside of my sports pants, filling my shoes and forming a puddle on the ground around me. I couldn't walk up to you. I couldn't ask what you were doing or who that woman was. It would have been too humiliating. I couldn't do anything but stand still, keep my balance by holding my bike and stare from a distance. People passing by looked at me and saw the puddle on the ground. One young man approached and asked if I was okay. I smiled weakly and waved him away. Yes, I was fine. I had only entered an alternate universe where nothing I believed made sense. I felt like I had fallen down a deep, dark well.

Now, however, I can look back and say that wetting my pants saved me. I am also grateful that only my bladder let go. It could have been much worse.

Over the years, I trusted you not to cheat because I loved you and believed in you. I believed in us. You still came home at night and you still made love to me often. I believed that we cared enough about each other to resist the temptation of becoming involved with anyone else. As far as I know, you were faithful until recently. If you weren't, I don't want to know.

I loved you. I still do; you are the man I have known and loved for thirty years. You are still so good in so many ways. I loved almost everything about you. I loved the sight, smell and sound of you. I adored having you near me. I loved who you were. I loved that because you loved me, you liked women in general, the same way that loving you made me respect what was good in all men. I loved our history and the possibilities for our future. I had been putting money away for a holiday on a luxury Great Barrier Reef island for your fiftieth birthday and I almost had enough saved before seeing you in the park. At the time, the idea of surprising you with a week on a tropical island was exciting. Now it just seems sad.

So I stood there in my wet pants, sodden socks and squelching shoes. I turned my bike around and headed home where I sat in the shower, cried for ages and went to bed, exhausted. The phone rang and I ignored it. I heard voices on the answering machine. My friends at the coffee shop were waiting for me. They all chimed in cheerfully together, wanting to know where I was, asking if I had forgotten, and to call them back. They were friends you hardly knew. When the kids were small, we all met at playgroup. We were still friends simply because we had known each other for more than twenty years. If I met them now, we would probably have nothing in common. Out of habit, however, and perhaps because I worried about what they might say about me behind my back if I stopped going, I met with them every second month at a café for gossip, trivial conversation, coffee and cake.

I lay in bed and listened to them telling me I was no fun and began to wonder who I could talk to about what had just happened. I knew with certainty it couldn't be any of them. It couldn't be any of my other friends either. I couldn't rely on any of them to understand, or to keep quiet about it. I missed Judy, my dearest and oldest friend. I could have told her and she would have understood, but she had been dead for two years, so there was nobody I could talk to about something that mattered so much.

Why didn't you say anything? I hear you ask. In my imagination, over the past ten months, I have heard you ask this question repeatedly. Each time you asked, I had a different answer, because I didn't know why I couldn't ask you about what I had seen. I was frightened. Initially, I was numb, paralyzed with terror. Everything around me was the same, yet different. I felt panicked and powerless. I couldn't think, let alone speak. All I could do was remember the way you shut down my phone call without the slightest interest in why I might be calling. Somehow that felt like a greater betrayal than kissing another woman in the park.

All I could do was ask myself questions that I was too afraid to answer.

What if I say nothing? What if I turn a blind eye? What if I just pretend that I don't know? What if I ask you? What if I confront you? What if you deny it and say it wasn't you and I was mistaken? What if you say you can't believe I could think you would do such a thing? What if you accuse me of being paranoid or suspicious?

What if you admit it? What if you say you love her? What if you say it's been going on for weeks, months or years? What if you say you want to leave me? What if you want a divorce? What if you say she is pregnant? What if you want to marry her?

What if I never see you again?

What if you come home and tell me you are leaving? What if you come home and tell me you want *me* to leave and tell me you never want to see me again and kick me out the front door? What if I have nowhere to go? What if you move that woman into my home once I am gone and she moves into my kitchen, into my bedroom, into my bed, into my life?

What if you convince the courts that the house is yours? What if I come home and the doors are locked and my suitcase is on the porch and that woman is inside, laughing at me, or pointing at me through the curtains? Or calling the police?

What if I have a nervous breakdown and lose my job and can't get another job because I am too old? What if I have no money and nowhere to live?

What if our kids like, no, love that woman more than me and she turns them against me and I never see them again? What if you have more children and you all spend happy Christmases together? What if I spend every Christmas alone? What if I am always alone, living in a caravan, on government assistance? What if I turn into a homeless, old bag lady who dies, cold and alone in the street and they find me days later, frozen to death?

What if, what if, what if.

Was I being melodramatic? Yes, when I think about it now, I definitely was, but at the time, I couldn't stop asking myself those terrifying, unanswerable questions. They invaded my mind like a swarm of wasps, one after the other. I didn't have answers for any of those questions. They made me frantic and unable to think rationally. Each 'what-if' was worse than the last. I could hardly breathe.

I couldn't stay still. I paced around the house, crying and babbling to myself like a mad woman until I was exhausted and had to lie down. Then I got up, paced and babbled until I was exhausted again and lay down. Eventually I wore myself out and curled up under the covers.

I don't suppose you remember, but I'll ask anyway. Do you remember the day you came home and I had the 'flu'? I was all hot and congested. I wouldn't let you look at me because you would have seen that I had been crying and wasn't really sick at all. That was the day I found out you were seeing another woman. That was the day I knew that my marriage, as I understood it, was over. When you brought me a cup of tea, I couldn't meet your eyes. I didn't notice then that you had trouble meeting mine. That came later.

You slept in another room that night so you wouldn't disturb me, or catch 'the bug'. I lay awake for hours. I could hear you snoring, so close and yet so far. I wanted to run to you and have you wrap me in your arms. I wanted to look at your beloved, sleeping face. But I didn't dare. I couldn't move from the bed so I reached across to your side. It was cold and empty. I put my face in your pillow to smell you, but I could smell perfume as well, and it wasn't mine. I rolled back onto my side of the bed and cried, trying to stifle the sound with a corner of the blanket in my mouth. Being in our bed without you was the loneliest place on the planet. If anybody had offered me a chance to die, I might have taken it. I eventually fell asleep. I dozed fitfully, my dreams were disturbing and I woke in a sweat. You left for work without waking me.

I stayed home that day and wandered aimlessly through the house, still crying and talking to myself and asking questions. What if you come home today to tell me you are leaving me? I spent the day pacing the house. I couldn't eat. I stopped wanting to think, because each thought became a frightening question, followed by another question that I couldn't answer. The faster I thought, the faster the questions came up and they went around and around in my head and wouldn't stop.

That night, when you came home from work, I was still in bed and you brought me a cup of tea. By then, I really did look unwell. There was a concerned expression on your face, which I interpreted, with pitiful hopefulness, as love. It gave me the chance to believe that perhaps you still loved me and that what I had seen the day before was temporary and unimportant.

But I didn't believe it was. There seemed to be such intimacy between the two of you, such affection and enjoyment. Your summary dismissal of my call was so immediate, so automatic. I knew your relationship with that woman wasn't a fling, but you looked at me that evening with something in your eyes that felt, to me, like love, and with that little ray of hope, I fell into a long, deep sleep. When I woke the next morning, I was certain I couldn't say anything to you yet. I had to wait. I needed some answers to my questions first.

But why didn't you say something? I hear you ask again. Why didn't *you*? I reply. Oh, I know the answer to that one. Why would you? You were a married man who believed he was getting away with having an affair and you didn't know I had seen you in the park.

Chapter 2

Twisting My Rings

The next morning I got up and went back to work. I had to. I didn't know what else to do. I didn't know where else to go. I only knew I couldn't stay at home alone anymore. If I did, I would go mad. The staff and the children at the childcare center behaved as they always had. Everything appeared normal, but I felt different. I felt bewildered and sick. I sat at the desk in my office and was desperate to feel normal again. Usually, I like to go and see the children, many of whom I have known almost since they were born. Our childcare center is a second home for most of them because their parents work full time, and as you know, I have always prided myself on knowing all their names and being able to find time to play with them.

That day, I stayed away from them. I stayed away from my staff. They took one look at me and stayed away from me as well. I sat in my office, staring at the papers on my desk. I couldn't make sense of anything in front of me. I couldn't focus, I couldn't think and I got nothing done.

As I walked along the corridor toward the staff room, a little girl called out to me. I stopped and squatted down beside her. She had a limp, forlorn, golden dandelion clutched in her little hand. She looked into my eyes, gave me the dandelion and said, "It's for you. Are you sad?"

"Do I look sad?" I asked her, taken aback.

"Yes," she said, "and Mummy says if somebody be's mean to you, use your words, then you be happy again." She patted my hand, smiled at me and turned to go. Her kindness and wisdom completely undid me. I ran blindly outside, hid in a corner and cried. If a small child could see that I was in a bad way, then others would too.

I needed help.

As soon as I could, I went back inside to the staff room. I trimmed the stem of the dandelion and put it in a glass of water, took it back to my office and placed it carefully on my desk. Dandelions have always been my favorite flower, beautiful, resilient and generally overlooked. They spring up optimistically in lawns after being mown down. They turn fields golden and their seeds float away like fairies on air currents, to find new places to grow. The flower is a perfect reflection of the sun and the seed head looks just like the full moon. Do you remember, Mike, how I often asked you to delay mowing the lawn so I could enjoy their sunny yellow heads just a little longer?

I looked at the little dandelion and thought about you. You had behaved almost normally that morning, although you paused slightly when I asked how you were. Why hadn't I noticed that before? How long had you been seeing her? I decided not to ask, but to wait. I thought you might wake up and end it or she might end it for you. For the rest of the day, I worked on budgets and employment policies, anything to get my mind off myself; anything to get my mind off you and that woman in the park.

When I got home that night, I fell apart. I dreaded your arrival home. I listened for the sound of your car in the driveway and your key in the front door. I sat in the dining room at my usual place, rocking, looking at my hands and twisting my rings. I thought, today he is coming home to tell me he has met someone else and he is leaving me. I sat there for a long time. Then, when I heard your car, I jumped up, ran to the kitchen, and started preparing dinner. You came inside and called, "Hi BB!" and went straight to the bedroom to change, something you had only recently started doing. I stared out the window and peeled potatoes. Jacques Brel was on the radio, singing 'Ne Me Quitte Pas'. I remembered enough of my high school French to know that he was pleading with someone not to leave him. It was a song of desperate promises. I had to turn it off because his pain, like mine, was so intense.

That weekend I told you I was 'taking it quietly after the flu.' I couldn't face going out or talking to anybody. You understood but had 'work at the office' both days that kept you away from me.

The following week I began to notice things I hadn't seen before. You looked at me only briefly when I spoke to you and your replies were a little off point. You went to another room if your phone rang. You made calls while you were in the yard or in the garage. You showered morning and night. For the first time in our marriage, you put your dirty clothes in the washing machine instead of leaving them on the floor or in the laundry basket. I resisted the urge to check the collars for lipstick. I resisted the urge to check your credit card statements, go through your suit pockets or do all the things that suspicious wives do. I resisted them all because I really didn't want to know. I knew enough. I just wanted to wait. I picked a dandelion from the garden, put it in a vase and sat it on the kitchen windowsill. I wanted to remember that 'if somebody be's mean, use your words, then you be happy again.' I was hoping a dandelion would give me the courage to talk to you. I was hoping a dandelion would make me happy again.

On Monday after work, I prepared the dinner and then sat in the dining room. I looked at my hands and twisted my rings. I kept thinking, today is the day he will come home to tell me he is leaving me. What will I do? I couldn't imagine doing anything other than crying and begging you not to go. I felt helpless and hopeless.

The following day was Valentine's Day. We had always done something fun and romantic on that day, but this year your card and gift were given with little thought. Your conversation was perfunctory. Your mind was evidently elsewhere. My heart ached.

Every evening, for the rest of that week, I sat in my chair and waited until you came home. When daylight faded, I sat in the dark, twisting my rings and waiting. I couldn't move. I couldn't listen to the radio anymore and I couldn't answer the telephone. I heard friends leaving messages but I couldn't speak to them. I would have to sound like my usual self and I couldn't.

The next weekend I tried to do what we usually did – housework, gardening and catching up with friends. Our lives were almost the same, but not quite. We did our chores and you went to play golf with Sam while I sat at home and waited. We went out with friends on the Saturday night. I began to feel a little better because you were attentive and funny. Then you mentioned to our friends that, because your company was branching into the inner-city residential market, you would be working more on weekends and in fact, you had a lot of work to do during the coming weeks. There was something in your voice that made my heart stop.

That night in bed, I looked at your sleeping face. That face was so familiar and so loved and yet now, it held secrets. You were probably dreaming about something I knew nothing about, something that had nothing to do with me. I was losing you.

The second week after I saw you in the park was almost the same as the first. Every day at home and at work, I put a dandelion in a glass of water to remind me to be courageous, like the lion in 'The Wizard of Oz', and to keep myself together for the staff and the children. Every night, I organized dinner and sat in the dining room in the dark. The house was silent and I held my breath, waiting for you to come home to me. I no longer asked myself those unanswerable questions. Instead, I began imagining unbearable possibilities. Every night I told myself that this is the day you will come home to tell me you are leaving me. This is the day you will tell me you have met someone else and are leaving me. *This* is the day you will tell me you love someone else and you want a divorce. After this day, I will never see you again.

Every night I imagined different scenarios:

I begged you not to go. I fell to my knees.

I told you that I loved you. I asked you if we could talk about it.

I asked you why. I made promises to change/improve.

I burst into tears. I sobbed uncontrollably.

I threatened to kill you. I threatened to kill myself.

I threw things at you and screamed.

I laughed hysterically. I yelled good riddance.

I said, okay, good, goodbye, go, your suitcase is already packed. Get a solicitor.

No matter what I said or did in these imagined scenarios, the outcome was always the same – you always left.

Every evening, when you came home, I panicked; I jumped up out of my chair and went to the kitchen. I pretended everything was fine but I was riddled with panic and pain. Sometimes you noticed I was unhappy and you assumed I was still grieving for my mother who died two months before, and I let you believe that. You would hug me briefly and then turn on the television for your daily dose of bad news from around the world.

One evening you looked intently at me, as though you had something to tell me, and my heart stood still. No, no, I thought, not yet. I am not ready. I don't want to hear it. I looked at you and you looked at me. You turned away to watch the news. How close did you come to saying something that I wasn't ready to hear? I didn't know why you stopped but I was glad you did. I wasn't ready to consider a different life.

Sometimes, you phoned from the office to say you would be working late. I asked if everything was alright and you replied that you were just very busy, so I said I would leave your dinner ready for you. Sometimes you said I needn't bother cooking for you, because you would eat at the office while you worked. Those were the most difficult evenings for me to get through. What was I going to do if I couldn't keep busy? Who was I if I wasn't your wife, making your dinner? I had no clue.

One afternoon during the third week, you rang to say that work was so busy you would take a hotel room in town for a few hours and go back to the office early in the morning. Your words were a punch in my stomach. The pain was unbearable. I hung up the phone and paced around the house. You weren't coming home at all. I would be alone. I walked through the house feeling restless and agitated. I paced like a caged animal. I turned on the television and turned it off again. I picked up the telephone and put it down again. I picked up a book and put it down again. I literally didn't know what to do with myself. I didn't want to go to a friend's house. I didn't want to stay at home alone. I didn't know what I wanted to do.

I felt a sudden urge to escape, so I picked up my handbag and keys and got in the car. I didn't know where I was going. I just drove. I saw the freeway and drove onto it. Before I realized it, I was fifty kilometers away. I left the freeway and found a motel, went to the front office and asked for a room. The young woman behind the counter noticed that I looked distressed and didn't have any luggage. She asked for identification and looked into my bag while I was trying to find my wallet. Maybe she thought I had come to kill myself. I didn't want a total stranger to worry, so I tried to smile reassuringly at her.

"It's okay," I said. "It was a last-minute decision. My husband and I had an argument. It's nothing serious."

She wasn't convinced. She gave me a room key and told me call her if I needed anything, anything at all. I thanked her, went to the room and lay on the bed. She called me an hour later, just to make sure everything was to my satisfaction. She sounded relieved to hear that I was alive and well. I wanted to sound cheerful for her sake, but I couldn't manage it.

I lay awake on the bed for hours, still fully clothed. I stared at the ceiling, imagining you and your girlfriend together, and realized I had come to an even lonelier place on the planet. The last time I saw the clock was just after three in the morning. I was woken by a call from the receptionist on duty at nine. She sounded relieved to hear my voice. I was alive, but exhausted, hungry and very cold. I rang work to say I would be late.

That night, after coming home, I sat in the dining room telling myself that I couldn't do this anymore. I promised myself that I would ask you. I said over and over: today I will ask him; today I will ask him, *today* I will ask him. Then, when you arrived home, I couldn't do it. I just couldn't.

If anyone had told me then, that I would feel as good as I do now, ten months later, I wouldn't have believed them. I *couldn't* have believed them. At that time, I couldn't have imagined my life without you. It was beyond me to even consider the possibility of living without you. You were the love of my life. You still are, and now I am leaving you.

A few nights later, I looked at the dandelion in the vase on the windowsill and managed to summon the courage to ask you if we were okay. You looked at me, startled. You asked me what I meant. I said that I could feel a distance between us and I wanted to know if everything was good between us. You told me that work was busy and you were just distracted. You told me not to worry and you hugged me. You hugged me longer than I hugged you. For the first time ever, I was the first to let go. For the rest of that evening, you paid close attention to me. You made me a cup of tea and sat with me on the couch while we watched our favorite television show 'The Big Bang Theory'. I was even able to laugh. Later, you made love to me tenderly, for the first time in a long while.

In some way, that made it worse. You loved me but you were seeing someone else. I couldn't get my head around it. I thought I was going insane. I needed to talk to someone and I knew it couldn't be you – not yet. It couldn't be our kids. Eleanor would be devastated and Henry, well, you know Henry.

It couldn't be any of my friends. I already knew what they would say and I knew what their words would mean.

Oh my God, how awful! *(How thrilling! I am so glad your life isn't perfect. Thank God it is you and not me.)*

Oh, you poor thing, tell me all about it. *(I want to know everything so I can tell the others.)*

How long have you known? *(Give me all the juicy details.)*

Who is the other woman? *(Anyone I know? I hope so, what a hoot!)*

Are you sure it was your husband you saw? Maybe you were mistaken. *(Wouldn't that be hilarious?)*

Don't worry, it's just about sex. (*What's he not getting at home?)*

How long has it been going on? *(Tell me more, give me all the dirt.)*

What are you going to do? *(Don't ask me to help. I don't want to get involved.)*

How are you going to survive? *(Can you still afford to be friends with us?)*

Get rid of the bastard. *(There was always something not right about how perfect he was.)*

Don't leave him, there's nobody better out there. *(Not for somebody as plain as you. You will die poor and all alone. Don't you know the odds of finding somebody decent once you're over forty?)*

Call me if you need anything. *(I'd love to stay and chat but I have to get the dog to the groomers.)*

Let's catch up soon. *(Don't expect me to invite you to dinner parties, because who invites single women? It just annoys the other wives. Maybe I could fit you in for a movie now and then. How soon can I get away to tell everyone? Catch you never.)*

Do I sound cynical? You bet I do, but I have seen them do it before. Don't you remember the Andersons?

Other than my Mum and Judy, your father was really the only person who could make me feel good. Very early in our relationship he took me aside and told me he thought I was 'a keeper'. He said he had married a keeper and had been perfectly happy for many years and he hoped you were wise enough to see that I was a keeper too. But I couldn't talk to him now. It would break his heart.

I had to find someone to talk to before I went out of my mind. It had to be someone I didn't know, someone I wouldn't have to make conversation with at a party sometime in the future. I thought of seeing someone professional but I didn't want some twenty-something, newly-graduated therapist with lots of theories and no life experience telling me how I should feel or what I should do. I wanted to talk to someone mature. I really wanted my Mum. I missed her more than at any other time in the two months since she died. I cried because she was no longer here. At the same time, I was glad she didn't know what was happening.

It didn't occur to me then that she might have known what you were doing. It didn't occur to me then that I might have been the only person who didn't know.

Chapter 3

A Desperate One-Time Thing

Going to see a psychologist was an act of desperation. I was afraid I was going mad. Jacques Brel's song played repeatedly in my head and I couldn't shake it. I wasn't sleeping and I could scarcely eat. I looked pale and tired and I was losing weight.

I had passed the sign many times on my way to work. *'Anne Holmes, Clinical Psychologist, By Appointment Only'* and a phone number. I decided to call her on my way home from work. I stopped my car outside her office and made the call. I hoped she would be an older person. I decided I would go to see her once, and no matter what happened, I would go *only* once. It wouldn't matter how tearful I was or what she thought of me because I would never see her again.

Anne Holmes answered the phone. She sounded like a sensible, older woman and I felt relieved. When she asked me why I wanted to see a psychologist, I whispered, "My husband is having an affair." I choked up and couldn't speak. She waited patiently and then said, "This sounds urgent," and gave me an appointment at 2pm the following day. After I ended the call, I had a terrible moment of panic because I had made your affair more real simply by saying it out loud. I cried a while longer, sitting in the car outside Anne Holmes' office. Then I settled down and told myself that if I could talk to her, it might help and maybe I would be okay.

What did I expect from a psychologist? I expected to lie on a couch and talk and have someone say, "Mmm, hmm" and "How does that make you feel?" I assumed I would have to talk about my childhood and all my problems. I would then be told what to do and that would be that. Little did I know there would be *so* much more to it.

Anne Holmes' office was in a house that had the front rooms converted into an office and a waiting room. I was apprehensive when I walked in. I was afraid of seeing someone I knew, but no one was there. I sat in a large armchair and looked around me. Almost immediately, the soft silence and the comfort of the room soothed me. There was a framed certificate on the wall that read 'Anne Holmes, Clinical Psychologist'.

Anne was a woman in her fifties. She was simply and elegantly dressed and had kind eyes. She smiled and held out her hand. She didn't seem to notice that my hand was sweaty when she shook it with her own warm, dry hand. I followed her into her office and she gestured me toward a comfortable armchair. I felt even less apprehensive when I saw there was no couch. Anne pointed to a jug of water and a glass on a coffee table between us and suggested I help myself. One wall of the room was lined with books. There were two armchairs, a desk with a CD player on it, an office chair, a filing cabinet and a cupboard. There was a pretty pot plant on the desk and beautiful paintings on the walls. One in particular caught my eye. To make conversation, I asked Anne about it.

"That's a Grandma Moses print," she said. "She is my inspiration. She didn't pick up a paintbrush until her late 70's when arthritis made it impossible for her to hold an embroidery needle. Her exhibitions broke attendance records all over the world."

"It's lovely," I said. I sat back and relaxed a little. I was in safe hands.

Anne pressed a button on the CD player, sat down and smiled at me as though she already knew me and liked me, which was comforting. "Have you ever been to a psychologist before?" she asked. "Any history of mental illness?"

I shook my head.

"Well then, where would you like to begin?"

I must have opened and shut my mouth like a fish because she smiled again and said, "Relax and breathe slowly. You will be okay, I promise. When you are ready, tell me briefly about yourself."

I told her that I had worked for years as a kindergarten teacher and now ran a childcare center four days a week, that I met you on a blind date when I was eighteen and you were twenty. We had been married for twenty-six years and had two children, Eleanor, twenty-four and Henry, twenty-two, and they both moved out two years ago. We lived in the house that was my parents' home. My widowed mother wanted to move into something smaller and offered us the house on our wedding day.

I told Anne that Eleanor was a florist while Henry was doing a master's degree in environmental science, and they were sharing a house with friends, close to the city. You were the director of a real estate company. On Wednesday mornings, I took care of your parents. My father died when I was a teenager, my best friend Judy died of cancer two years ago and my mother died only recently. Lastly, I told her that we had to have our lovable old Labrador, Molly, put down one month ago.

Unexpectedly, I started to cry and was soon sobbing. I was crying for Judy, for my Mum and Dad and for Molly. I was crying for myself. Anne leaned forward and moved a box of tissues closer to me. I grabbed a handful. She said nothing but sat and waited. Her presence was soothing. I didn't feel that she was trying to be sympathetic. I loathe sympathy. I can't stand it when people pity me.

Anne wasn't sorry for me. She wasn't even sad for me. She didn't join me in my misery. She just waited patiently until I was ready to talk. She gave me the impression that she had seen it all before, that I was not alone, that my situation could be easily fixed and that in fact, all was well.

After a while, I blew my nose and made those remarks that women make when they know they have made themselves ugly. I wanted to comb my hair and wipe my eyes and I wished I hadn't worn mascara. When Anne passed me a small mirror, I looked at my wretched reflection and tried to clean up some of the mess. All that crying had given me a headache. I needed to go to the toilet urgently and while I was there, I looked at my watch and realized I had been crying for some time. I returned to my chair and looked at the floor. Anne poured me a glass of water and encouraged me to drink.

I told her that I had seen you in a park with another woman and that because I knew you and loved you, I was sure you weren't having a meaningless fling. You were not a flirt or a philanderer. It was probably a serious thing for you. During our marriage, I had never suspected that you might be with another woman. I told Anne that I had spent nearly two days in bed and then three weeks unable to decide what to do. I told her I couldn't ask you about it and when she asked me why not, I said I was afraid that you would leave me. I told her about all my terrible 'what if' questions and about how I was unable to answer any of them.

"How are you feeling?" Anne asked.

"Um, I feel like I am at the bottom of a deep, dark well," I replied.

"You need a ladder to get yourself out," she said, nodding. "Tell me, what do you want?"

"I don't want to lose my husband…"

Anne interrupted quickly, saying, "I didn't ask you what you *don't* want, I asked you what you want."

I stared at her. I didn't understand the distinction.

She continued. "If you focus on what you don't want, you get more of what you don't want. Start again. I want…"

I started again. "I want to keep my husband?" I felt like a child trying to get the lesson right for the teacher.

"You want to keep your husband. Good. Why?"

"Why?"

"Yes that's right, why do you want to keep him?"

"Because I love him and we have been happy for a long time and I don't want…"

Anne raised her hand to interrupt. "Don't add that. Just tell me what you want."

"I want to keep my husband. . ."

"Because…?"

"Because we have been married for twenty-six years and we have been happy and I want to stay happy and…"

"You want to keep him because you want more of the same. That's understandable."

"Yes, yes I do. I wanted it to last forever."

"Until death do you part?" asked Anne.

"Yes, exactly, exactly…I wanted us to grow old together." I then noticed I had spoken in the past tense and my voice drifted off. My heart sank.

The enormity of what I might be losing, my husband, my home, my family, my past and my future, overwhelmed me. I started to cry again. Anne sat back, waiting.

I am having trouble writing this, Mike, because it was an awful time for me. But I really want you to know how I felt in those first few weeks so you will understand why I am doing what I'm doing today.

After what seemed like forever, I was able to settle down.

"You probably think I shouldn't feel this way," I said. "You probably think I'm pathetic. I know I do."

"Firstly," replied Anne, "what *I* think needs to be irrelevant to you and secondly, you need to make peace with how you are feeling now. You are where you are and that's okay. You have to begin from where you are." She paused. "Are you suicidal?"

"No! No, I'm not," I said. I stared at her, a little shocked. Could she tell I had thought about it?

Anne looked at me intently so I admitted to her that in the first few days I had wished I were dead. I believed that if I didn't have you, I had no reason to live at all. Some mornings I thought I would prefer not to wake up, but I didn't have any plans to kill myself. I mentioned the acute despair I felt that night in the motel. If I was ever going to kill myself, it might have been then, but I didn't, so I probably wouldn't now.

Anne smiled and said, "Good. I had to ask. The only way you can begin to feel better is to be okay with how you are feeling now. It doesn't mean that you will always feel that way. I don't think being miserable is your default setting. To me, you look like a person who is usually happy, but today you are feeling scared, powerless, isolated, desperate…" She smiled. "Stop me if I get this wrong."

Despite myself, I smiled. "Yes I am feeling that way, and some!"

"The most seductive emotion we can feel is self-pity," said Anne. "It can encourage us to be a victim. It can also make us want attention and sympathy from our friends."

"But I loathe sympathy!" I objected.

"Good. That's important," replied Anne. "Your job is to find ways to feel better about your situation and my job is to help you do that. I don't give advice, I don't give sympathy and I am not just a sounding board for your complaints. I am going to support and challenge you and all your decisions will be yours. How does that sound?"

I was a bit dazed but I nodded to indicate that it sounded okay.

"Therapy is about learning to think and feel better, no matter what the circumstances are," said Anne. "If you don't believe that's possible, read 'Man's Search for Meaning' by Victor Frankl. Therapy helps you recognize which thoughts sabotage you and which thoughts lift your mood. My job is to help you find feelings that help you make good decisions. Any decisions you make while you feel as you do now, will be decisions you regret.

"Therapy doesn't end in this office either. At home or work, I want you to do everything you can think of to make yourself feel a little better. I want you to be careful about what conversations you have, what music you listen to, what television shows and movies you watch. Choose things that lift your mood, just a little. You will begin to notice what has a positive effect. Eliminate the rest. You don't need other people's dramas. Also, get out more, walk in the sunshine, go to the beach. Get some exercise. It all serves to make you feel better. Now, tell me briefly about the night you spent at the motel. What did you think about?"

"I lay there and thought about them talking and laughing and kissing in the park and going out for dinner. I imagined them going to bed together, I tortured myself…." I had to stop there. I couldn't breathe.

"You focused on what you didn't want and dug yourself deeper into that well," said Anne.

"Yes," I said, "and then I started asking, how could this be happening to me, why this is happening to me, what I did to deserve this, and that made me feel terrible. Then I thought about how happy I had been before I saw them in the park. I mean, Mike and I had just had our twenty-sixth wedding anniversary. We went to a lovely place for dinner and everything seemed nice between us. I thought we were happy. I like being married. It gives me such a feeling of belonging. When you see the other person's face, you smile inside and think, ah, there you are, and it feels safe and warm. I can't bear the thought that it has gone and I don't know why."

Anne folded her arms in front of her, as though ready to hear more of my story. "So now, tell me about the parts of your life that are okay. What are the positive aspects of your life?"

I looked at her, bewildered.

"What do you love about your kids?" she asked.

I was taken aback by the unexpected questions. I didn't think I could shift my focus from something so bad to something else that was better. I took a deep breath and sipped some water.

"Um, our kids are great. Eleanor is the funniest thing, bright as a button and the best daughter anyone could ask for. She loves her work, she visits about once a fortnight and always has a funny story to tell me."

"What is your favorite memory of her?" asked Anne.

I remembered an image of our darling daughter.

"She was about six years old and ready to go to a party dressed as a dragon fly."

Do you remember that, Mike? She danced about, flapped her wings and insisted we take her photograph again and again.

"She was so beautiful and so happy. She loved the costume I made. One of the photographs is still on the fridge."

"And Henry?"

I hesitated. Henry went through a rebellious, angry adolescence and worried us terribly. I remembered him yelling at me and calling me a moron.

"Henry went through a tough phase…."

"Don't go there. Tell me what is positive about him now," said Anne.

"But I thought the point of going to a psychologist was to talk about problems!" I said. I was confused.

"That's not the way I work." replied Anne. "Tell me what's great about Henry now."

I thought for a moment and started again. "Henry has matured into an intense young man who follows the beat of his own anti-establishment, save-the-planet drum. He plays the tin whistle beautifully." I smiled at a recent memory of him and Anne smiled too.

"Keep going," she said. "Tell me more about Eleanor and Henry."

Soon, I was talking happily about the kids we both love. I had forgotten all about you. Anne kept asking questions, encouraging me to tell her about the funny or clever things they had said or done. I showed her the photos I kept in my wallet and told her about their kindergarten drawings and photos that were still on the fridge and the kitchen pin board. When I was talking about our kids, I was happy. Anne asked me to notice that I was happy, really notice it, and to use those memories as a way to start feeling better every time my mood dropped low. She suggested that whenever I began thinking about you and your girlfriend, I could choose to remember what I loved about Eleanor and Henry, or Molly, or anything else that made me smile.

"Therapy is work," said Anne, "and sometimes it is hard work. Occasionally, I might give you homework. It requires you to be focused and honest and to know exactly what you want. I have recorded this session so that you can listen to it again later. Can you record on your phone?"

I nodded and she continued. "In future sessions, I would like you to record our sessions so you can go over our conversations later in your own time. I would also like you to start writing in a journal. It will help you become aware of your own thoughts."

I nodded again. This was not going to be a one-time act of desperation after all. Anne passed me a card with a new appointment time for the following week. Then she took a CD out of the machine on her desk, put it in a paper sleeve and handed it to me. I left, feeling a little better. I felt a strange kind of relief. The dark shadow of despair that loomed over me had shifted to a softer grey.

Later, when I returned home, for the first time in weeks, I didn't sit in the dining room in the dark, looking at my hands, twisting my rings and waiting for you to come home. I didn't sit there, wondering when my life as I had known and loved it, would end. Instead, I sat at the kitchen bench and looked at the family photos and drawings on the fridge and the pin board. I looked at the little dandelion on the windowsill. I was feeling just a tiny bit better.

Chapter 4

The Art Of Tweaking

I was longer waiting for an axe to fall. I went to work. I got on with my to-do lists and kept myself busy. Some nights, you came home early, other nights you were late and once you didn't come home at all. I stayed home that night. I sorted out the laundry and linen cupboards until I was exhausted because I didn't want to lie awake in bed thinking about you. I put your pillows down the middle of the bed to create the illusion that you were there, which helped me feel safe and less alone.

I went back to see Anne. After I settled into my chair, she reminded me that I had finished my first session by talking about the positive aspects of our kids. She asked how I had been during the week and I told her I had tried to think of positive things, but sometimes, especially in your company, it was difficult to do. When you looked at me, my heart soared with hope and when you looked away, it stood still. I kept wishing that I could wake up and find it was all a bad dream. Anne then asked me to think about the kids again, and to think about what it was about them that made me happy.

I told her that the sight and sound of Eleanor and Henry made me feel fifteen years younger. I felt needed, appreciated and still relevant. I stopped at the words 'still relevant'. I needed to catch my breath because something in my chest was hurting. Anne asked me if I had felt the tug, the 'turning upstream' of those last words. I didn't know what she meant by turning upstream but I had felt the pain. She explained that thoughts and words are powerful, that every thought we think and every word we speak has a physical and emotional effect on us. She asked me to imagine taking a boat down to the edge of a stream, getting into it and pushing myself away from the shore with a paddle. I could turn upstream and paddle hard against the current, or I could let the momentum of the current take me downstream.

"Which would feel better?" she asked. "To paddle hard upstream, or allow your boat to take you gently downstream?"

"Downstream sounds good."

Anne nodded and continued. "Thoughts that make us feel worse are called upstream thoughts because they make us feel like we are battling against a strong current. Downstream thoughts are those that give us a feeling of relief, as though we are floating gently downstream."

"Like the song," I said.

"Exactly," she replied. "Imagine that everything you want is waiting for you downstream and you are happily drifting toward it. How did the words 'still relevant' make you feel?"

When I explained that they made me melancholy, Anne suggested there was an underlying thought behind those words and asked me what it was. I told her I didn't know, but she gently insisted that I did.

"I don't know!" I objected.

"Yes, you do. You said that when you see Eleanor and Henry, you feel 'still relevant'." She made quotation marks in the air with her fingers. "What does that mean? I am going to challenge you on this."

I could feel something rise inside me – a thought or fear that I didn't want to acknowledge.

Anne said in a soothing voice, "It will be okay. You can do this. I am right here with you. I won't let you fall."

Her gentleness disarmed me. I couldn't speak.

Anne persisted. "So what is the thought?"

I looked at her, wide-eyed, and whispered. "What if I'm not relevant to anyone anymore?"

"Is that how you feel?"

I nodded, trying without success, not to cry. I felt irrelevant to my kids, I felt irrelevant to you. I felt that I mattered to nobody in the entire world.

You know how much I hate crying. I hate the way it makes me swollen, snotty and sweaty. I've never understood why crying makes me sweat but it does. Do you remember our first date when you took me to see the movie 'Terms of Endearment'? I cried through most of it and you had to take me home to shower and change my clothes. I was sure you would never ask me out again. I was surprised you even wanted to wait while I changed. You looked through the books in my bookcase and then took me out to dinner. You said, "I'd better never make you cry." I said that perhaps you should re-think your choice of movies for a first date and that maybe a Steve Martin comedy would be better. On our next date, we saw him in 'The Lonely Guy', which made me laugh *and* cry.

Once again, in front of Anne, I cried. I became red, swollen, snotty and sweaty. Anne sat quietly and passed me a box of tissues and put a waste basket near my chair. This time, I took the box and kept it on my lap. She asked me whether I was really irrelevant or was that just a thought. I told her the kids didn't need me anymore. I missed the days when Eleanor and Henry would sit around the kitchen bench or in front of the television with their friends, eating junk food, talking happily and making a mess. I missed the times when Molly would hang around me in the kitchen, banging the backs of my knees with her wagging tail, waiting and watching for bits of food that might fall onto the floor, hoping for a pat and a scratch or the offer of a walk. I missed your arrival home when you would come up behind me, pat my butt, kiss me on the neck and ask how my day had been.

The house had been alive and I was a part of it; I was needed. My children needed me then, but they didn't need me anymore. Molly was gone and she didn't need me and now, apparently, neither did you. Anne asked me again if that was a thought I kept thinking. I said the kids have their own lives now and I don't see them as often as I would like.

"Ah, good," she said. "A statement we can do something with: 'I don't see them as often as I would like.' Is there anything you could do about that?"

I hesitated. "Maybe I could invite them over more often, but they're always so busy. What if they say no? Oh, is that just a thought I keep thinking?"

"Yes, it is, clever girl! It's good to work with someone who can pick this up quickly. It is only a thought and thoughts can be changed."

I felt a small glow of pride, as if I had done something smart and the teacher was pleased with me. I was pleased with myself.

"You really torture yourself with those what-if questions, don't you!" said Anne. "Your unanswered what-if questions give you so much pain. You need to learn how to answer those questions or ask different questions. How could you resolve this fear that Eleanor and Henry no longer need you?"

"I could ask them for dinner?"

"Are you asking for my approval?" Anne laughed.

I repeated emphatically, "I could ask them for dinner."

"What might get in the way of you asking them?" said Anne.

I wanted to cry again but Anne nipped it in the bud by reminding me firmly to breathe. I took a deep breath, held it and let it go slowly. I was worried that if the kids came for dinner, they would notice you weren't there. They might ask where you were and I would have to lie. I didn't want to lie to them.

"Don't hold your breath," said Anne. "Breathe and keep your throat open, let the emotions escape on your breath. Don't hold them down."

I breathed slowly and it worked. The emotional surge dissolved like the foam on a wave.

"What might get in the way?" I asked. "They might say yes, and see their dad is not home. They might also say no."

"And that would mean…?" said Anne.

"That they are busy."

"And?"

"That they don't have time to see me. They may not want to see me." I could feel the surge again and breathed it slowly away.

"And? Go for it."

"That they don't love me." I said plaintively.

"And that means?"

"That I was a bad mother…." I whispered.

I didn't know where that thought came from. I believed I had been quite a good mother, not a perfect Women's Weekly kind of mother, but a good one all the same. You often told me what a good mother I was. I was astonished to find that I thought differently.

"Is that a thought you keep thinking?" asked Anne.

"If it is, I didn't know I thought it!" I exclaimed.

"But it was back there all the time. Is it true?"

"What?"

"Were you a bad mother?"

"I don't know. I don't think so." I paused. "Maybe I blamed myself for the way Henry was as a teenager. Maybe I thought it was my fault. Of course, if I knew then what I know now, I might have done things differently..."

Anne held up her hand to stop me talking.

"There's a strategy that might be useful for you. When you think a negative thought like, 'I was a bad mother', you can add a word to it that softens it a little, a word that gives it a slightly different meaning and evokes a different feeling. It's called tweaking. For example, you can add 'sometimes' to 'life is hard'. 'Life is hard sometimes' doesn't arouse the feelings of suffering and defeat that 'Life is hard' does, does it?"

I repeated 'Life is hard' and then modified it with 'sometimes', and I could feel the difference. However, I didn't know how I was going to tweak being a bad mother.

Anne continued, "The thought that you were a bad mother is unnecessarily harsh. It sounds to me like you did a good job of raising your children. So let's tweak that thought. I was a bad mother...?" She looked at me with an intent gaze.

"I was a bad mother .... sometimes?"

I didn't know what else to say. This tweaking thing was entirely new to me and I wasn't sure how it worked. I said it again, "I was a bad mother sometimes."

Anne smiled at me and I continued, "I was an okay mother sometimes too! I was a damned good mother sometimes too! I love them!"

"I know you do. Remember," said Anne. "I am helping you become aware of thoughts that might be creating resistance to inviting them over for dinner, that's all. Repeat after me and breathe... I was a good mother."

I repeated it.

"They have busy lives and they love me."

"They have busy lives but they love me," I said.

Anne held up her hand again.

"Don't create resistance with the 'but'. Say after me. They have busy lives AND they love me."

I repeated it.

"If they ask me where their dad is, I will say he is at work."

I repeated it.

"How are you feeling now?" asked Anne.

"Better," I replied. I really was. I felt like a small burden had been lifted.

"And don't forget these two things," said Anne. "Beliefs are just thoughts you keep thinking and it is important that you feel good, because that feeling will spread outward like ripples on a pond and those near you will also feel good."

Chapter 5

Holding My Breath

I could invite the kids for dinner more often. If they said they were busy, it would be okay because I could ask them again another time. It would also be okay because I was a good enough mother. When I went home, I sent them an email and gave them a range of dates they could choose from to come over for dinner. I promised them their favorite meal, roast lamb with all the trimmings; cauliflower cheese, gravy, baked potatoes, pumpkin and beans and a dessert of caramel custard and cream. I received two prompt replies and we settled on a date that suited us all.

You were there for that dinner, Mike. It was lovely. I forgot for a while that you were seeing someone else. For one evening, I could imagine we were still a happy couple with two wonderful children. It was easier than I thought it would be and yet, when I looked at them and then at you, I wanted to cry.

That night, you reached for me in your sleep and held me close. You murmured my name and my heart thumped in my chest. I lay awake, hopeful, doubtful and hopeful again. I was afraid to cry in case I woke you. You still loved me. I felt grief and relief all at once. The next morning you told me you had a conference in Sydney for three days the following week, and the nightmare returned. Nothing had changed; you were behaving like a guilty man. I wanted to ask you not to go, to plead with you, to threaten you, to hit you and tell you to stop being such a fool. I wanted you to wake up to what you were risking, but I couldn't do anything except hold my breath and hope that my pain would go away.

One night, while you were in Sydney, I went out for dinner by myself because I couldn't be bothered cooking for myself. I went to a local restaurant and asked for a table for one. I was uncomfortable and embarrassed. I imagined everyone was looking at me and feeling sorry for me. I felt like Steve Martin in 'The Lonely Guy'. I kept my eyes on my plate, ate quickly, then left as soon as I was done, and decided I never wanted to do it again. After arriving home, I took Anne's advice and did something to make myself feel better. I went onto YouTube and watched that particular scene in the movie and it made me smile.

Why didn't you say anything? I hear you ask. What was I going to say? I saw you in the park with someone else? I know you've been lying to me for weeks? Then what? I couldn't bear the thought of you possibly saying, yes, I've met someone. I'm in love. I want a divorce. It would mean you didn't love me anymore and that you were prepared to give up everything we had. It would mean I would never see you again. I wasn't ready to hear it. I was afraid I would collapse and die from the pain of knowing that I would never see you or touch you again.

I didn't say anything because you still came home most nights and while you did, I wanted to believe that I was still in the race.

Eleanor and Henry came for dinner during the week you were in Sydney. They were sorry you weren't there and so was I. We seldom had 'all-family' dinners anymore but you were away, presumably with that woman, while we were at home, and I made the best of it. We got out the photo albums and enjoyed remembering all the happy times we'd had. Sometimes they asked me questions about a photo because they couldn't remember the actual event. Helping them remember made me feel good. Then they looked at our wedding album and laughed at our fashions.

Eleanor looked at the photo of you and me and said, "You and Dad have been together a long time, haven't you!"

"Yes," I said distractedly. "We were."

"You were?" Eleanor looked startled.

"I mean, yes, we have been," I replied.

Eleanor looked at me intently and I looked away. I didn't know what to say.

I was looking at a photo of our bridal party, smiling at the camera. We all looked so young. We were almost unrecognizable. Back then, my hair was very long and you still had all of yours. We looked so joyful, so expectant of happy times ahead. For the most part, we were right. Your sister Amanda looked lovely as my bridesmaid. Sam was there too, smiling seductively at the camera. He couldn't help himself. He had to flirt with everyone and everything. He flirted with the assurance of a man who knew he was both handsome and charming. He flirted with me, even at our wedding. He stood behind you at the altar, looking at me with soulful eyes that said that he couldn't believe I was marrying you when I could have had him. I ignored him.

When you first introduced him as your best friend, he flirted outrageously with me. I treated him with amused disdain. That piqued his pride and it became a challenge for him to win me over. Back then, he was already cheating on his first wife with a woman at work. I thought he was an immoral jerk and I was worried when you went into business with him, but apparently, he knew exactly what he was doing when it came to business. Over the years, he kept up his barrage of charm but tried a more subtle approach, which amused me even more. He was never able to dent my armor though. I loved you too much. I didn't think that he even really fancied me. He was just jealous of you because you had a happy marriage.

I told the kids I had something in my eye. I went to get a handkerchief and spent quite some time getting that 'something' out. I felt Eleanor watching me. I knew she suspected that I was unhappy. I gave her reassuring hugs, because I didn't want her to worry. She was close to you and she would also feel abandoned by you if she knew what was happening. She would be angry and hurt and I wanted to spare her that pain. Did you realize that you would be hurting her too?

Two weeks later, at my next appointment with Anne, I felt angry and irritable. What we were doing was not changing anything. You were still having an affair. I had practiced her ideas about thoughts and I was writing in my journal, but she was not telling me what to do to keep you. I was beginning to think I was wasting my time. I was also annoyed at how calm Anne always was. She never seemed to get upset. I asked her why she didn't get upset when I was.

"Because I wouldn't be able to help you if I did," she said. "While you're focusing on the problem, I focus on the solution. Solutions aren't found in the same place as problems."

She reminded me that the thoughts I think create the way I feel and that I can choose my thoughts. I can control it all. Inwardly I scoffed at the idea. I sat looking at her, thinking, I don't control my thoughts, my thoughts control me! I was really annoyed.

Anne continued. "Understand that when you think of Michael, you can still choose to feel good." She noticed me bristle at the mention of you. I didn't want to be made to feel worse. I had cried enough. "You could choose to think of the positive aspects of him," she said.

I retorted that I couldn't think of *any* positive aspects of you, not one. Just thinking about you at all made me feel miserable and angry.

"Notice those feelings and ask yourself, 'Do I want to feel this way?' If the answer is no, turn your thoughts in a different direction."

"Do you mean, just think of something else?"

"Yes that's exactly what I mean. At this point, that's about all you *can* do. You're not ready to write a list of his positive aspects or to take any action, are you, other than what you are doing?"

"No," I sighed. "You're right. I'm not. I can't find a good thing to say about him and I am not ready to confront him."

"Or to leave him," Anne added.

"Or…to leave him," I whispered.

I told Anne I was living my life tip-toeing around you, holding my breath, suspended between fear and anger. I couldn't confront you because you might leave me. I was acting as though I hadn't noticed the change in you, but how could I know and love you and *not* notice the change in you? The change in your face, your voice, your touch, your smell, your routine, your showers, your leaving and arriving, your trips away? Even your new ties! How could I not notice?

Husbands have cheated on wives since the dawn of time and marriage. Books have been written and films have been made ad nauseam about it, but do you know something, darling? I didn't think it would happen to us. I really didn't think you would be that stupid. I mean, seriously; to fall for a girl twenty years younger than you, who is probably looking for a husband to give her children before her biological clock runs out?! She must be how old? Thirty? Has she told you she doesn't want children? I'll bet, within a year, she 'accidentally' falls pregnant. Is that what you want? Do you really want to start all over again with dirty nappies, mess, sleepless nights and parent-teacher interviews? Do you really want to organize a twenty-first birthday party when you are seventy-two years old? I know you, my darling Mike. I might be wrong, but I don't think you do.

Despondently, I watched my feet and avoided Anne's gaze. I was unsettled by her talk of me leaving you. That had never occurred to me.

"Look at me," Anne said.

I lifted my head. She looked at me in a way that felt unconditionally, yet impersonally, loving.

"Repeat after me, I can choose thoughts that help me feel better."

I repeated it.

"I choose thoughts so I can feel better no matter what he does."

I stared at her and she stared back, so I repeated it. "I choose thoughts so I can feel better no matter what he does." I didn't believe it for a second, not one word of it.

I whined at Anne.

"Why do I have to do this? Why do I have to be the one who changes?"

"Your work here is to move up the emotional ladder until you are on a rung where you can climb out of that well," Anne replied.

"An emotional ladder?" I exclaimed. "I thought I was paddling my boat in a stream!"

"Yes, you are right," said Anne ruefully. "I may be using too many metaphors. Let's start with the emotional ladder. When I first saw you, you described yourself as being at the bottom of a well, so I thought the image of a ladder would be helpful. Each rung of the ladder represents an emotion like fear, sadness, rage, revenge, anger, all the way up to exhilaration, appreciation, joy and passion.

"The stream metaphor was to help you recognize whether your thoughts made you feel better or worse. So if it is okay with you," she said, "I would like to continue using both those metaphors."

I told her it was okay with me and I would let her know when I was confused. In the meantime, I continued to whine and complain.

"I can't shake the feeling that if I had been different somehow, more interesting, more sexy, more funny, more of everything, he wouldn't have had an affair. Maybe I was smug, lazy or boring. Maybe I neglected him or took him for granted, or all of the above."

"How does it feel when you blame yourself?" asked Anne.

"Awful. It makes me feel guilty."

"Then don't blame yourself. Just blame him. Blame feels better than guilt. You will feel better."

"I'd rather blame *her*," I said. "I just want him to stop seeing her!"

"Well, with the way things are, you can't change anything he does, so the best thing you can do is watch with interest what he does."

"But I *want* to change what he is doing! I want to *stop* what he is doing!" I moaned.

"And how is that working out?"

"It's not." I felt defeated.

"Then let's keep doing what's working. Enjoy your work, enjoy your kids and look for things to appreciate."

Yeah, right! I was living with a man who was sneaking around behind my back, lying to me daily, sleeping with someone else, and I was supposed to smell the roses! I told myself that the next time I saw Anne would definitely be the last time. I would give her just one more chance to solve my problem.

Chapter 6

Spitting Venom

I went back to see Anne a week later. It had not been a good week. I was angry now and prepared to admit it. I didn't want any of this thought-changing nonsense. None of this 'you are in a well or in a stream' or whatever. No more 'beliefs are just thoughts you keep thinking and you can change your thoughts'. Nothing had changed. I was furious.

Anne settled into her armchair and asked me how I was feeling. I replied that I felt very angry.

"Rage is good," she said, smiling.

"Huh?" I stared at her.

"Rage is good. It means you're not scared anymore. Is that right?"

"Yes! I am *not* scared anymore. I don't keep running that stupid scenario through my head where he comes home and tells me he is leaving and I fall into a sobbing heap. I am not sad or scared anymore. I'm furious!"

"Good. Now show me how mad you can get." Anne sat back and looked speculatively at me. Suddenly I felt afraid. I have always been scared of people in a rage. I have always tried to avoid confrontations with them. Enraged people are ugly and frightening. They hurt people.

"But why?" I asked. "How can getting mad possibly be better than being scared?" I tried to sound indignant because Anne was going in a new direction. I was afraid to follow. I thought she was trying to turn me into one of those women I'd read about who cut up their husband's clothes and stalk their girlfriends. I didn't want to be one of those women who give validity to the saying that 'Hell hath no fury like a woman scorned'. I told Anne that I did not want to bitch about the bastard who had ditched me for some young bimbo. She watched me steadily, calmly and with a glint of amusement in her eyes.

"Well, that was easier than I thought it would be," she said. "How did that feel?"

"Awful. I hate it. I would hate to be one of those..."

Anne held her hand up. "You think there is more virtue in being sad and scared than being enraged, but sadness has no power. Fear has no power. It's time you got your power back."

"I don't agree," I said. "Rage feels pretty out of control to me. It's like a toddler having a tantrum because she is powerless to change what is going on around her. I don't want to do that."

"That's my point precisely," replied Anne. "While you wait for Michael to tell you he's leaving, you *are* powerless; you are giving him all the power. You are making everything dependent on what *he* does. You are paralyzing yourself. Getting really angry will help loosen up that paralysis."

I felt like pleading with Anne. Never had I felt so at odds with her. I began to wish I hadn't come back. I wanted to get up and walk out of there, but I didn't know what I would do without her support.

"But I've seen women like that," I argued. "All they do is rage about their husbands or ex-husbands and the other women. They don't stop for days, weeks, months and sometimes for years! Their friends get tired of listening to them. They start avoiding them. I don't want to be like that. I don't want to be just another bitter ex-wife."

"I understand that," said Anne, smiling, "but those women got *stuck* in rage. There is nothing wrong with *arriving* there. The trick is not to stay there, but to move through it, past it, towards something else."

"What else?"

"How about frustration, hope and joy? Think of it as climbing up your emotional ladder out of that well, one step at a time. Now, I want you to go for it. Get furious. You showed me a little of it before and it was impressive. Let's go back to that bit about the bastard and the bimbo. That was a good spot."

I stared at her in disbelief.

"Get mad. Let's burst your rage balloon," Anne persisted. "You have one chance and one chance only to say it out loud."

I was dismayed. You know me, getting angry really isn't my thing. I've done it, you've seen it and you know I don't like the out-of-control, spitting, venomous feeling of rage. Rage is scary. Rage is when people say things they really mean, but later have to pretend they didn't mean, because what they said was so cruel or foul.

"I can't," I said.

"Are you worried about what I'll think of you?"

"Maybe," I replied. I meant, definitely.

"Oh, so you want to stay stuck, sad and scared and sorry for yourself?" Anne's mocking, pitying look made me furious. I wanted to hit her.

"How the hell would *you* feel if the man you loved for thirty years was cheating on you with some manipulative, scheming bitch? If he took away everything you loved for some conniving little slut!"

Anne smiled, which infuriated me more. It really got me started and then, I said it all. You were a loathsome, lying asshole and *she* was a whore. The two of you should get terrible diseases, die painful deaths and rot in hell. You would have been shocked. I spewed everything I thought about you and that woman and how the two of you had ruined my life. Whenever I slowed down, Anne said, "Is that all you've got?" I continued ranting until I couldn't think of anything else to say, and then I sat back, exhausted. I said everything I'd thought in my darkest hours. I listened to the recording later and I couldn't believe so many loathsome things had come out of my mouth.

Anne sat back, smiled and said, "Bravo! You had a lot of momentum behind that rage that might have tripped you up for years to come. Now, breathe. Feel that tremble in your body and let it go. Emotion is like vibration. Breathe it away."

I could feel it; it was like a train running through me. I couldn't move or breathe without trembling. My whole body was buzzing. I told her about it while I avoided her gaze. I was ashamed of what I had said. How could she possibly like me after that? What if she asked me to leave? What if she didn't want to work with me anymore? What if that meant losing you?

"What was all that?" Anne asked and gave me her 'I know you know the answer' look.

"Just thoughts I keep thinking?"

"Bravo again – and?"

"Thoughts can be changed?"

"Yes! Well done!" She sat back and waited while I drank a glass of water. Spitting venom was thirsty work.

I couldn't believe that Anne was so pleased with me for saying such terrible things. She didn't mind that I spat at her everything I was thinking about you and your girlfriend. She didn't flinch at any of the language I used, and I used the worst I could think of. She just waited for me to calm down and then said something that has saved me several times since then.

"There is only one rule. You can *never* do that again with another living person present, nobody, not once, ever. Not even with me."

"Why? I mean okay, but why?"

"Remember those women you were talking about earlier who were stuck in rage?" she asked.

"Yes?"

"Well, they felt rage and fed it to their friends who fed it back to them and they got caught up in the attention, the sympathy and pity-parties. If you can promise yourself that you will never say those words aloud to another person, you can avoid all that. You won't give rage any momentum."

I didn't know then what Anne meant by momentum, but it was a word I would hear often, and one I understood and appreciated fully, months later.

"What about when I'm by myself?" I asked.

"Sure you can," Anne replied, "but be careful what power you generate. When you have an angry thought, tell yourself to save it for your own personal rage party later. Tell yourself 'I don't have to think about that now. I can choose to think about something else. I can choose to give momentum to a good-feeling thought. I can set an intention to think better feeling thoughts'."

"Most mornings," I replied, "when I wake up, I go straight back to feeling angry, like a dog with a bone. I think I get some sort of masochistic pleasure out of feeling that twisting in my gut."

"However," said Anne, "you could wake up each morning and set an intention to feel better and enjoy yourself. In fact, at night you could set an intention to wake up and feel good."

"Even if nothing has changed?" I asked.

"*Especially* if nothing has changed," said Anne "So, now you have learned that thinking negative thoughts makes you feel bad."

"Yes, so I had better watch my thoughts."

"No, you had better watch your feelings and then choose thoughts that give you relief, and you had better watch your words around others. You cannot whine, moan, groan, complain, gossip or bitch and feel better. Negative words just entrench the negative feelings further."

Anne told me to plan a rage party for a particular time of the day when I was alone, and to time myself for ten minutes and then stop. I was to take note of how I felt and then either tweak my thoughts or find other thoughts that made me feel a little bit better. Not a lot better.

"Quantum leaps don't work," she said. "Aim to feel a little bit better, just one step up the emotional ladder."

Anne also told me that I wasn't allowed to tell anyone about you until I could do it with appreciation and joy. Like that's ever going to happen, I thought grimly.

I went home and had a ten-minute rage party. I did it twice in three days. I listened to the recording of my session with Anne to get in the mood. I ranted and raved, and then the steam just went out of it. The third time I tried, I felt stupid. I even giggled. The rage had gone, and in its place, there was a tiny granule of something that felt interesting, but unsettling.

Chapter 7

Writing Lists

At our next session, I told Anne I'd had two rage parties but I didn't feel like doing it anymore.

"So the rage has morphed into revenge – right?" Anne smiled.

"Yes! How did you know? I can hardly think of anything else," I said.

I was astonished that she knew what I was thinking and feeling. It also made me think that perhaps my new reactions were normal. I mean, if a psychologist knew I was going to feel that way, maybe that's what normal people feel in my situation. That idea lifted my mood immediately.

"Now we have to be careful not to let the momentum of revenge carry you," said Anne.

"Huh?"

"Well, you have created a momentum. It's like being on one of those roundabouts that children ride in a park."

I looked at Anne and waited. She was giving me another metaphor.

"Think of the movement of one of those roundabouts," she said. "You run and push hard to get it moving, then you jump on and it turns by itself for a while. It moves of its own accord and you can choose to stay on or jump off. If you make it go too fast, it will throw you off into the bushes.

If you let someone else control the speed, it may throw you off even faster and you could get hurt. Have you ever noticed that if you have a thought, another similar one appears quickly after it?"

I said that I had. No sooner had I thought of something that made me furious than another similar thought showed up.

"Be careful about getting revenge momentum going. If you want to think vengeful thoughts, think funny ones."

Funny ones? There's nothing funny about revenge. Revenge is mean, hateful and vindictive.

"Like what?" I asked.

"How about doing a pee on the seat of his car?" Anne smiled and winked at me conspiratorially, and I laughed.

It was hilarious that Anne, so calm and mature, could suggest something so ridiculous. I imagined myself squatting over your car seat, happily urinating all over it. Now that's funny, I thought.

Anne looked at me and laughed. "No hesitation at all... Simply remember that revenge can be fun and satisfying to *imagine or think about*, but *doing* something vengeful starts a momentum that will throw you off the roundabout and you will get hurt. Remember, we are talking about *thought* here, not action."

"So I can't really pee on his seat?" I looked at her, playfully.

"What do you think?" She paused. "When you find yourself contemplating revenge, I want you to turn your attention to something more positive, such as the things you have that the girlfriend doesn't have."

"That's easy. I have Eleanor and Henry. I have a long and happy history with him," I said.

"That's right. Now go and write a list of those positive things and bring it to the next session."

I left Anne's office and thought about what she had said. She wanted a list of everything I had that your girlfriend didn't have. You know I enjoy writing lists. I have a list for Wednesdays when I look after your parents, I have shopping lists, I have house repair lists and I have lists for tasks I need to do at work. I was happy that Anne asked me to write lists, except when she wanted me to write a list of your positive aspects. I wasn't ready to write that one. I wasn't anywhere near ready.

But there was something else I couldn't resist doing. I wanted to make a list of all the vengeful thoughts I'd had over the past week. I wanted to write them all down, look at them, and think of more. I didn't think Anne would approve, but I wanted to do it anyway. I thought it would be okay if I just wrote down acts of revenge and then threw the list away, so I went to a cafe with a notepad and pen.

Why didn't you say anything by then? I hear you ask. I didn't because I didn't want to, Mike. I was thinking mean and vengeful thoughts. I had turned to the dark side. I was on that roundabout and it was moving fast.

Chapter 8

Counting The Ways

Ahh, revenge, how much do I love it? Let me count the ways.

I sat in the café with a latte and a muffin and started writing a list of all the hateful things I wanted to do to you and your girlfriend. When I ran out of ideas, I leaned over to the next table and asked another woman who was also alone, if she could help me come up with some nasty things to do to an unfaithful husband. She looked at me as though I was some kind of crazy lady so I quickly told her I was writing a novel. She asked me the title so I thought even more quickly and said it was called 'Getting Even'.

She smiled and came to sit beside me. Then she came up with some vengeful acts that I would never have thought of. We were like co-conspirators in a thriller novel. It was great fun. After we had another cappuccino together, I thanked her and she left. She looked pleased about having helped an author. It then occurred to me that maybe she was in a similar situation in her life. I hoped I hadn't given her any terrible ideas that she would act on. She might not have somebody like Anne Holmes to talk to.

Together, we had thought of many horrible things that would cause you and your girlfriend humiliation and pain. We thought of hiring a private detective to take photos of you together and uploading them to Facebook, sending an email to everyone on your business contact list, telling them about your affair, and sending surveillance photos to your family and friends. We also thought of hiring a computer hacker to get into your whore's account so I could send something horrible to everyone she knew.

Then there was keying, slashing or crashing your car, or hers, and splashing paint over it, burning it, hammering nails into all four tires, throwing your beloved football memorabilia in the bin, putting dog poop in all your shoes, turning Eleanor and Henry against you, poisoning you slowly and crippling you financially. I kept writing.

I felt a spiteful glee imagining you outside our front door with one small, battered, brown suitcase (it had to be small, battered and brown, I don't know why), with no money and a maxed-out credit card (which of course I had maxed out). You banged on the door, begging to be let in and I refused. I was too busy jumping around, punching the air, yelling "Yes!" I was victorious. I imagined you arriving at your girlfriend's house and her not being pleased to see you.

You were supposed to be her knight in shining armor, ready, willing and able to rescue her from spinsterhood and poverty and whisk her off to a beautiful home in a quiet, green suburb where she could satisfy her urge to reproduce. She let you in, but she was obviously dismayed. She thought you were worth at least a million and you turned up at her place in debt. She started planning to get rid of you...

I looked over what I had written. I had created a list of fiendishly horrible things to do to you both. The list included stalking, terrorizing, torture and even, in my darkest moments, murder. At one point, I tried to decide which vengeful scheme to carry out. I wanted it to be one that would do you the most harm while giving me the most satisfaction.

Then, with a gasp, I snapped out of it. Anne's warning about momentum came back to me. I read the list through and was shocked and ashamed that I could go to such a deep, dark and vile place with so little prompting and with so much enthusiasm. I lost sight of myself as a nice, decent person. I realized I was capable of doing terrible things and that was scary. I quickly understood how scorned lovers could do such violent things to their ex-partners. On the other hand, making that list was so empowering.

I grabbed my pen and underlined the acts of revenge that were funny, and scribbled over those that were just appalling. I weeded out the ideas that took me to the dark side from those that made me feel lighter and that made me laugh. For example, I got a real laugh out of imagining your penis turning green and falling off. I didn't have to do anything and it was delightfully vengeful. I discovered that an occasional funny, vengeful thought felt fine, as long as I kept it to less than a few seconds. If I contemplated it any longer than that, another vengeful thought joined it. I was beginning to understand what Anne had meant about momentum.

I took the list home with me. On the way, I went to a DVD store and asked the woman behind the counter for movies about women whose husbands or partners had cheated on them. She looked at me, smiled and said, "Let's go look, shall we?" We found 'The First Wives Club', a BBC series called 'The Politician's Wife', 'Under the Tuscan Sun' and 'Belonging'. I took them all. The woman promised to keep an eye out for others that might interest me.

The next time you didn't come home, I watched 'The First Wives Club' and got into the spirit of it. Revenge can be entertaining when it's carried out by Goldie Hawn, Diane Keaton and Bette Midler. I laughed at Ivana Trump's line, "Don't get mad; get everything." I rewound the scene several times and added the thought to my list. I watched 'Under the Tuscan Sun' and was horrified to see how quickly the wife said, "Oh, she wants my house because it's near schools? Oh, okay then, I will just go away and she can have my house, my husband and my life!" Not that she used those words exactly, but it's what she did. There was no way I was going to do that.

I watched 'The Politician's Wife' and enjoyed the carefully measured destruction of her husband's career. It was fun to watch but I didn't want to do that to you. I didn't know how to go about it and it looked like too much hard work. The movie 'Belonging' was painfully sad. Brenda Blethyn was sublime as the abandoned wife. In the last line of that movie, she admitted that after she had lost everything and had established a new life, she was still terrified. I didn't want that either. I went to the library and looked for books with the same theme. I read 'A Summer without Men' and afterward I knew I was not going to go mad. I was going to be okay.

I burned the revenge list in the back yard and watched the smoke drift away into the evening sky. I picked a little dandelion and took it inside. In the end, there wasn't a single thing on that list that I might really have done to you or that woman. But there was one bit of sweet revenge I did carry out. It wasn't even on my list...and it was all her fault.

Chapter 9

Revenge Is Sweet

Not long afterward, I came home early from work. I walked through the side gate and into the back garden where I caught sight of a young woman sitting on the back patio. I stopped and looked at her. I had seen her before. She was that woman in the park, your girlfriend. She hadn't heard me arrive so I stayed still and stared. She was sitting in the late afternoon sun, looking out across our garden as though she belonged there. She had a peaceful, contented look on her face and it occurred to me that she was imagining herself at home.

But she was at *my* home, MY home, where I had grown up, where you and I were married, where Eleanor and Henry were conceived and where we had been happy, until she came along. Our lovely old home was built in the days when blocks of land were big enough for gardens and sandpits and cubby houses. Plane trees were planted on the nature strips. Those trees are so old now that they meet in the middle above the road to form a shady canopy in summer and create stunning color and delight for children in autumn. Some of my favorite photos are of the children playing in huge piles of fallen leaves that you and I were trying to rake up to burn. I still remember the sound and smell of burning leaves, even though it became illegal to burn them many years ago.

I approached the woman and asked her who she was and what she was doing there. She jumped up in fright. She had obviously thought I wouldn't be there at that time of day. She had probably planned to sit and mentally acquire my house and garden and then disappear before I arrived. She looked nervous. I could smell her perfume which was familiar. Feelings of rage and revenge began to stir.

She didn't know I had seen her before. She didn't know I knew who she was and what she was doing with my husband. She introduced herself as your personal assistant and said she was waiting for you with some important papers, but I didn't believe that for a second. At our home? Why not at the office? She wasn't very bright if that was the only excuse she could come up with. I heard her name but I didn't take it in. I heard the initials FC, which I thought suited her. Yes, I thought, I shall call you The FC. You can decide what you think they mean, Mike. Whatever you decide, you're probably right.

She was a woman in her early thirties, dressed for work in a dark suit. She had the sort of build that becomes fat in middle age (thick wrists and ankles). She was nice looking I suppose, if you like that sort of thing, which you obviously do, but she was not as good-looking as I had remembered, possibly because I'd only seen her from a distance and since then, my anxious imagination had taken over. Up close, I could see the dark regrowth in her shoulder-length bottle blonde hair. She had it teased into a small mound at the front of her head, which reminded me of a cassowary. She drew lip-liner just a little too high up on her top lip. She was wearing high heels that made her much taller than me.

We inspected each other. She looked at me with growing confidence. Of course, she would. I am an ordinary-looking, middle-aged woman, neither fat, nor thin, neither beautiful nor ugly. I became a little thicker around the middle after the children were born, but not much, and in the past two months, I lost most of it.

You always called me your little brown bird. You told me early in our relationship that the most beautiful songs are sung by small brown birds – nightingales, lyrebirds, thrushes, sparrows and bellbirds. I am not exotic, not a head-turner, you said, but there is a definite beauty in brown birds. I thought you were being so romantic and as long as you called me *your* little brown bird, your BB, I was happy. Actually, the best that could ever be said about my appearance was something a former boyfriend once said. He told me I 'scrubbed up well'.

Do you remember when we were set up for a blind date by friends at university, and you asked them if I was good-looking? They said I had a nice personality, which, as we both know, meant that I wasn't *that* good-looking. When you first saw me, you looked mildly disappointed, but as we talked more, your appreciation grew. I was used to that reaction. I knew exactly how good-looking I was or wasn't. I had no illusions and I still don't. However, from the FC's perspective, I was old and plain and you deserved much better. You deserved her. She looked me up and down, taking in my sensible low heels and my ordinary working-day clothes that allow me to sit on the floor with children. When she looked back up into my eyes, there was arrogance and contempt in hers.

What did you tell her about me, Mike? Did you use the standard line that your wife doesn't love or understand you, doesn't appreciate you, won't sleep with you, is cheating on you or is as dumb as soup? Did you tell her I was boring in bed? Did you tell her that I was an unfeeling bitch, a cow, a nag, a waste of space? What on earth could you have said about me that would make her look at me like that? What made her so confident that she could come to *my* home and pretend it was hers? How could she possibly think that *you* were already hers? She looked at me as though I was a bad smell that had turned up at *her* home.

I became determined to wipe that look off her face. I wanted to make her feel nervous again. I looked at her and thought, I wish you were dead. Vengeful thoughts were gaining momentum and I remembered something Anne had said. Make it fun. Swinging a chainsaw at her would have been fun, cutting her into little pieces and using her as fertilizer for my roses would have been fun.

Instead, I invited her in for a coffee.

I gathered my thoughts by turning to default. Offer the guest a beverage (thank you, Sheldon). I suggested that she wait for you. When she declined, I insisted. "It won't take long to make a coffee," I said, "and it will be nice for us to get to know each other. After all, you work with my husband." In the end, she could hardly refuse. I was sweet, so very sweet.

Reluctantly, she followed me inside and I went to fill the kettle. I breathed deeply, to keep myself together. I stood rigidly at the sink and stared out the window to give myself time to plan my next move. The FC wandered to the mantelpiece over the fireplace to look at our photographs. I turned and watched as her eyes roamed around the room and I knew she was imagining how she would change it when she lived there. Maybe she had been there before. I couldn't bear the thought that you might already have brought her to our home. Had she been in my bed? That would have been the worst betrayal of all. The idea of her living in my home sucked the breath out of me. I leaned forward to get mugs out of the cupboard and to give myself time to recover.

Then as the kettle boiled, I realized I had the perfect opportunity for some exquisite revenge. I loved you. I wanted to keep you. You were mine. I badly wanted to hurt her, beat her and defeat her then and there. I wanted to stomp her into the ground, or crush her and bury the pieces, but I couldn't do anything that she might complain to you about. I didn't want to be the one who looked bad, so I couldn't give her a black eye, but I could do something else, something that was much more effective and a lot more fun.

I gave her a mug of coffee and we sat up on the stools at the kitchen bench. When she put her hands around the mug, I noticed her finger nails were like long, bright orange claws. They had small decorations on the last two that looked like Easter eggs, and I wondered why any grown woman would spend so much time and money on something that made her look so idiotic and immature. Didn't she know that only dumb bimbos have nails like that? Didn't she know that it is more important to be able to do things like hold pens, use keyboards, turn keys, open car doors, wash dishes and put on pantyhose? The money she spent on her nails would probably feed a family for a year. Did her nails make it easier for her to pick her nose or insert a tampon? Did she find it difficult to wipe her butt? Did men look at those nails and worry about the safety of their crown jewels? I stopped looking at her nails and got back into the battle. Round one to me – she was definitely stupid.

I told her it was lovely to have her company because you were away so much lately. I told her you were often out in the evenings and that tonight, you would be out again. She blinked hard and I saw that this was news to her. Just a little of the self-assurance went from her eyes. I told her that you had worked late *every* night that week and I could see her thinking, *Every night? But I only saw him twice.* I told her you were working so hard because, only *yesterday*, we were making plans for your early retirement and we were hoping to live somewhere warmer, near the sea, for your arthritis.

"It got so much worse last winter," I confided.

"Arthritis?" she asked. I enjoyed the brief glimpse of dismay on her face.

"Oh yes, he goes to such lengths to hide it, poor love," I explained, "but one of his knees is just about ready for replacement. He is starting to have prostate problems too. Apparently, that happens a lot to men when they hit their fifties. Oh, I probably shouldn't tell you that. After all, he is your boss." I saw that blink again and I felt a quick frisson of satisfaction.

I told her how much we were looking forward to becoming grandparents. At our age, we were hoping that our kids would settle down and have babies. I gushed about how you will make a terrific grandfather. I even confided how, only a week ago, I thought I was pregnant again, at forty eight, like John Travolta's wife Kelly Preston, but the doctor told me it was menopause. I gave her that conspiratorial us-girls kind of wink and mentioned that you were very relieved that I wasn't pregnant because, as you said, you were too old and certainly didn't want to go through *that* again.

I glimpsed her confusion and disgust, which answered a question I had. You must have told her we didn't sleep together anymore. I thought, if she thinks that's disgusting, wait until she hears this! I told her that the doctor was concerned about a genital itch I had and he took a swab for pathology. I watched her cringe. I was beginning to enjoy myself. I had the exquisite pleasure of seeing her arrogance disappear and doubt and revulsion take its place.

Oh, how lovely is subtle, innocent-seeming revenge. I made you sound middle-aged, even old, a potentially arthritic cripple, imminently incontinent and impotent, forgetful and sweetly boring. I exaggerated only slightly. Maybe I overdid it. I don't care. It was fun. It was also liberating because, for the first time in my life, I didn't care what someone thought of me. I didn't care whether she thought I was old, plain or boring, because if I was, then maybe you were too. Maybe she would realize that you were just putting on a show for her, and that I represented who you really were. Maybe she would see you differently enough to want to dump you.

She asked me how long we had lived in this house and I raved on about what a long and happy marriage we were having here. I told her that both of the children were conceived here. I wanted her to imagine the two of us having sex together and I wanted that image to make her skin crawl. I took the children's photos from the fridge and pin board.

"Henry looks exactly like my husband did twenty-two years ago and this is our daughter Eleanor who must be about your age." I pushed the photos under her nose and made her look closely.

I said that we had lived in this house for "longer than you've been alive, dear" and watched her heart sink. I knew that she was dying to get away to phone you and find out where you were, but she wouldn't be able to reach you. She didn't know what I knew. Henry had called me to say that the two of you had made a last-minute decision to go out for dinner and watch a football match. I knew that you always turned your phone off when you watched football so you wouldn't be disturbed.

That was mean, I hear you say. Yep, deliciously mean, I reply, but don't forget, she is sleeping with *my* husband. She had the nerve to come to *my* home. She asked for it. Actually, I think I handled it rather well. I was polite. I was friendly. I even invited her to your fiftieth birthday party and droned on about your fortieth, thirtieth and twenty-first birthday parties, all of which I was at. I told her how lovely it was to know someone for so long "and I hope you can find that with someone too, dear."

I went on and on until I was sure she was ready to tear her hair out, or mine, and I hadn't said one mean thing. After about an hour, she left, saying she couldn't wait any more. She was leaving because she couldn't take any more. She didn't leave any important papers. I took a deep breath and thought, mission accomplished. Her arrogance and self-assurance had gone. This battle was mine. I almost felt sorry for her.

After she left, I was elated and trembling. It was probably nervous exhaustion but it felt fabulous. All the vicious revenge fantasies I had been harboring vanished. It was as though the rage and revenge had burned clean and left nothing but a clear plan. I had met the enemy, I had faced her and I knew her weaknesses. I was no longer scared, I was no longer enraged and I no longer wanted revenge. I was angry.

Weren't you already angry? I hear you ask. No. That was rage, this was anger. The rage I had felt was out of control, blind and unthinking. It's why we use the term road rage and not road anger. Rage is what makes a man take a baseball bat to a stranger's car in traffic, while anger makes him plan a different route to work. Anger feels better; it feels more powerful. I was angry now and I felt clear-minded. I had a definite goal.

I wanted my life back and I was going to fight for it. I wanted to keep what I loved. I wanted that stupid, bottle-blonde bimbo with claws to go away. I wanted to keep you. I loved you. The FC was just a passing phase, just a mid-life crisis, like a new red sports car, and I could cope with a red sports car. It was just a temporary madness, a forgivable, temporary madness. I would wait it out, and I would keep what I loved.

I wanted my life back, but I didn't know how or where to start. After the FC had left, I looked at my to-do list on the kitchen pin board and sighed. There were already so many things I should do that I didn't really feel like doing, so I took the list down. The first thing I did was clean out all my bedroom drawers and cupboards. Don't ask me why. It just felt like the best place to start. I went through my bedroom closet like a fiend. I threw out everything I didn't like and everything that didn't fit or that I'd had for years. Dresses, shirts, pants, coats and shoes were thrown into black plastic garbage bags and put in the boot of my car, and old underwear went in the rubbish bin. It felt so good.

Then I sat down with a coffee and wrote the list that Anne had wanted me to write. It was calming and a little anticlimactic. I wrote a list of the positive aspects of our lives together. I wrote about our history, our children, our shared sense of humor, our favorite activities, our love-making, our companionship, our extended families and our good friends. I definitely had some advantages that the FC didn't havc. You and I grew up singing the same songs, going to the same concerts, watching the same television shows. We both adored 'The Big Bang Theory' and often quoted from it. We understood each other's allusions. We almost had a secret language of our own. We could look at each other at a party or over a dinner table and know what the other was thinking. We knew each other well and loved what we knew.

That night when you arrived home from the football match, I was sitting up in bed, pretending to read. You started getting ready for bed while telling me about the game. You told me who won and who lost, but I wasn't paying attention. I was still buzzing with silent exhilaration and some nervousness about what might happen next. I thought I was ready.

You went to the bathroom to brush your teeth.

"Oh, by the way," I called, "Your assistant dropped by today."

You stood still. I could feel the pause and the silence.

"She did? She came here?" You were stalling for time, so you could answer and sound only mildly interested.

"Yes, at about four this afternoon. I found her in the back yard on the patio. Nice young girl – about Eleanor's age?"

Another pause. More silence.

"A bit older than Eleanor," you called. I smiled wryly at that.

"What did she want?" you asked.

"To give you some papers she thought were important. Forgetful though. She didn't have any papers with her."

I sat there thinking, come in and tell me about it. I dare you, Mike. I am ready for you, I think.

More silence.

You came back into the bedroom and looked at me intently while I stared at my book, seeing nothing. You got into bed.

"Why were you home early? Are you okay?" you asked.

"Yes, I had a headache, but I am good now."

"That's not like you. You don't get headaches."

"No," I said, "It's not like me at all."

I put down my book, kissed you quickly, rolled away from you and turned off my light. I thought, 'Chainsaw'. That made me smile. You said good night and turned off your light. I knew from your breathing that you were awake for a very long time. That made me smile too.

Chapter 10

Power Is Good

For a couple of days you were more attentive than usual. You even put out the rubbish bins without me reminding you. I imagined you asking her what on earth she thought she was doing coming to your home. Maybe you confronted her

.

Maybe you were angry with her. *Were you trying to get me caught?*

Or maybe you were saying to her: *Are you okay, my darling? I didn't expect her to be home at that time of day, yes, of course I'm leaving her! Yes, it's just not the right time; her mother has just died. Any day now, we will be together, I promise.*

Maybe you waited to see if she would tell you that she had been at our house. Maybe she waited to see if you knew. Was anything said? That question consumed me for days but I wasn't to find out for another eight months.

Every day after the FC's visit, I expected to see a change in you, anything that would indicate that she had decided you were too old for her and had dumped you, but it didn't happen. Perhaps she wanted my house too much. Whatever the reason, she didn't give you up. She probably thought I was pathetic, going on about you, while all the time you were telling her that you were leaving me. I thought that maybe you would dump her, but perhaps she looked at you with big, apologetic, adoring eyes. Maybe she gave really good head. Whatever it was, nothing changed. You were away just as often and you were home late most nights. Occasionally, I caught you looking at me with love and concern. My heart and breath would catch and I would feel hope again, but it was brief and became less frequent. You stopped touching me. You were away more often. You came home smelling, sounding and looking different and my heart cracked a little more, and still I couldn't say anything.

At my next session, early in May, Anne let me know that she was taking a six-week holiday. She would be rafting down the Colorado River in America with friends. I was nervous about her being away for so long, so she gave me the name of someone else I could talk to, if things became difficult for me. I told her I would rather wait. I confessed to her that I had written a revenge list and how equally fabulous and awful it made me feel. I also told her about my revenge against your girlfriend at our house, how I decided to call her the FC, how the experience made me a little giddy with power and how that feeling quickly faded when I realized that it hadn't changed anything. I asked her how feeling better solves anything at all.

"How does it feel to make a decision when you're happy?" asked Anne.

"Well, the decision feels right, so it's easy," I replied.

"Then, only make decisions when you feel good. Get happy first, and then make a decision. In fact, don't do anything until you feel good."

"But this isn't helping me. Nothing has changed. He is still having an affair! And now I am too angry to say anything."

"How do you feel when you think about him?"

"Angry and frustrated," I sighed.

"Not ready to write a list of his positive aspects?"

"Not even close."

“You’re frustrated,” she said, “notice how that feels.”

“It’s hard to breathe.”

“So stop and breathe.” I sat still and began the breathing process Anne had taught me, keeping my throat open to allow the emotion to flow out. I calmed down a little.

“What’s the thought?” Anne asked.

“If I spoke to him, I’d be so angry, I would leave and find myself out on the road looking for a motel, not knowing what to do or where to go. Then the FC would move into my home.”

“How would that feel?”

“Powerless.”

“How would you like to feel?” asked Anne.

“Power…ful?”

“And what would make you feel powerful?”

“Telling him, no, this is my home and I am not moving out. It was my parents’ home before it was ours and there is no way I am moving out and letting *that bitch* move in and take over my life! I grew up in that home. I was married in the garden of that home. Our children were conceived in that home. Our memories are in that home. It is *my* home.”

“Are your memories in that house or in your head?” asked Anne.

“Umm, in my head.” I hesitated.

“Okay, so tell me how you feel,” said Anne.

“About what?”

"Your home."

"I love it," I said. "I relax when I come in the front door because it's where I can be myself. It makes me feel alive; it has absorbed my childhood memories and my children's memories. Our bedroom holds memories of when our children were conceived and many great nights, mornings and afternoons."

"Keep going."

"I love the garden. It had swings and a cubby house and later it had a trampoline where I played and sat with my friends and a big bowl of chips. Later still, my friends and I camped out in the garden. We secretly drank UDL's and hid the cans from my parents. Then it happened all over again for my own children, years later."

"And it all makes you feel…?"

"My home, I know I should say *our* home, but I really want to say *my* home. My home makes me feel safe and loved."

"They are good feelings. Do you think you could have those feelings anywhere else?"

I stared at Anne and I could feel the resistant tug in my body.

"No! That's my home. It's mine!"

"Is it? Legally, I mean? Did your mother leave it to you or both of you?"

"Actually, she left it to Eleanor and Henry." I immediately felt the hurt that I felt when I found out that my Mum had changed her will. It had been so unexpected and so inexplicable.

"Why do you think she did that?" Anne looked a little puzzled.

"I don't know. I was shocked at the time. I only know she changed her will not long before she died."

I hadn't spoken to you or the kids about Mum's will. I had been very hurt by her decision to bypass me, her only child, and I didn't want to talk about it until I understood it. You weren't there for the reading of the will you just assumed that the house was now ours. For whatever reason, we had never discussed it. Copies of the will were provided for Eleanor and Henry as the benefactors, but they left them with me, unread. It didn't occur to them that the house would be left to anybody but me. So guess what, darling, surprise, surprise, the house is not yours or mine. It's not ours. It belongs to the kids. I didn't tell them because I didn't want to give them the chance to sell it and take it away from us.

"How do you feel about the house belonging to Eleanor and Henry?" asked Anne.

"I was hurt and confused at the time. It has just occurred to me that maybe Mum knew something I didn't. Do you think that's possible?"

"Yes, it's possible," said Anne. "But we will never know, so what are you hoping for now?"

"Now I'm hoping we can stay there for as long as we need to and then either Eleanor or Henry will live in it when we've gone. Maybe they will love it the way I love it."

"Or maybe they won't. That's not in your power to control, is it?" said Anne.

"No, it isn't. They might decide to sell it and divide the money between them." I felt discouraged.

"Yes, they might," said Anne. "As I said, you don't have the power to control what your children do." She leaned forward. "Many people misunderstand the meaning of the word 'power'. Power simply means having the ability to make choices, to choose what you want and to understand why you want it. Power equals freedom to choose, that's all."

"So it's okay for me to want to feel powerful?"

"How does it feel to be powerless?" asked Anne.

"It's the worst feeling in the world."

"So how can being powerless be a good thing?"

"It can't. I get it. I got it."

"Good," said Anne. "Now, tell me what makes a good childcare center?"

Another question from out of left field. I told her about some of my ideas regarding the center and Anne nodded agreeably. "There could be a good book in that," she said.

Chapter 11

Paddling Upstream

Almost every day for the next six weeks, while Anne was away, I looked at the list of what I had and what the FC didn't have. I thought that when Anne asked me to write this particular list, I was supposed to do something with it. It wasn't until long afterward I understood that writing the list was just meant to make me feel better, and wasn't a list of things to do. I wish I had known that earlier. However, at the time I thought it was a list of what I had to work on, to change and improve. Anne was away and I couldn't ask her, so I set to work on the list.

It was the most intense, concentrated effort I have ever put into anything. I concentrated on it at work and at home. I thought about it all the time. I tried to eliminate my annoying habits. I didn't sing or whistle around the house. I always replaced the lid of the toothpaste, and opened the milk cartons on the right side. I was trying to be perfect and it was exhausting. I probably wasn't much fun to be around. I was driven by my determination to keep you because I believed we could come through this. I believed that either you would realize you were an idiot, or she would realize you were an idiot. As it turns out, I was the idiot.

Firstly, we had friends. Didn't you notice we saw them more often? Didn't you notice that for a while we had more dinner parties? I could see you resented me organizing them, even when it was for our oldest friends. You were disinterested in the arrangements, distracted when our friends or family were with us and relieved when they left, but I couldn't help myself. I thought I was supposed to work on everything I could think of to keep you.

We had a long, loving history. I thought we knew each other well. Why didn't you notice the change in me? Couldn't you see I was no longer the calm, happy person I used to be? Why didn't you notice the strain I was under, trying to do everything right? Why didn't you notice I had lost weight and had become too thin? Were you so totally consumed by that woman that you didn't notice I was suffering, or did you deliberately ignore it?

We had a lovely home. Didn't you notice that I had cleaned out all the cupboards, rearranged all our belongings neatly and kept everything tidy? Didn't you notice how hard I was working to clean and organize every cupboard, every drawer, every corner, every cabinet and every room? Everything we were ever given or had ever bought was neatly arranged where it should be.

We had children. Didn't you notice the regularity with which they came to dinner? Didn't you notice that I made your favorite meals and tried new recipes? No, you didn't. How could you? You were home so seldom. Most of that food became leftovers for me to take to work or for the Eleanor and Henry to take home.

We had relatives. We were part of a larger community of people that included parents, aunts, uncles and cousins. Your parents needed more care. Didn't you appreciate that I was helping them stay independent by doing their housework, their shopping and banking? I was the one who took them out for drives and afternoon teas in the country.

We had things in common. Didn't you notice that I invited you to go cycling, to watch our favorite shows, to go to the comedy festival or to eat out at your favorite restaurants? We had an active sex life, pre-FC. Didn't you notice my new negligees? Didn't you notice my new energy? No, you didn't. Of course you didn't. You were usually too tired at night and I couldn't bear to think why.

I was doing everything to keep you. It was all I could think of. There seemed to be no other possible alternative. But now when I look back, I realize that our lives were not really all that exciting, or even interesting. We were ordinary people. I am not a celebrity, a scientist or a bright light on the social stage. I am a childcare center manager who comes home with funny little stories about the children I work with. I have no intellectual insights to share with you, no witty repartee, and you are an ordinary man, an estate agent who likes to play golf and watch football on television. I never expected our lives to be exciting and apparently, neither did you. I never heard you suggest we climb the Himalayas, or sell everything and sail a yacht around the world.

We were two ordinary, suburban people living our lives the way most people live their lives. We took camping and golfing holidays. When the children were small, we went to the same beach resort each summer and saw the same people who were also having the same holiday, year after year. There's not much adventure in that, I think now.

My last attempt to keep you was when I arranged the party for your fiftieth birthday. You told me you didn't want a big event, but I didn't listen. Silly me. I went ahead and sent invitations to family, friends and your colleagues. I spent days buying and cooking food and I ordered champagne and a cake. I had Henry take you out for the afternoon while Eleanor and I prepared the house. By the evening, I was exhausted. I wanted everything to be so perfect. I wanted you to be surrounded by people you had known and loved for a long time. I desperately wanted you to see what you would lose if you left me for that woman.

I had asked the FC to come, when she was at our house. I hadn't meant it; I didn't want her there. I didn't think she would have the nerve to come, but I was on tenterhooks all day and I didn't start to relax until halfway through the night, when it was clear that she was not going to show up. Henry brought your parents with him. They sat together on the couch and smiled at everyone. They looked old and frail. Your sister Amanda came down from Sydney for the party and spent much of her time looking after them.

I wished my mother was there because I really needed someone on my side. I ran around with trays of food, which gave me something to do. There was no one there, other than the kids and your father, that I particularly wanted to talk to. One good thing about being the hostess was that I had a good excuse not to talk to anyone for long. There were fifty people in the room to celebrate you and watch you blow out the candles, and nobody knew I was suffering.

Sam was there. His young trophy wife number three was flirting with Henry's friends out on the patio. Sam said nice things about you in his speech and we toasted you. Then you gave a speech. You thanked your parents and your children. You thanked everyone for coming. You then turned to me, the first time you had spoken to me that evening, and thanked me particularly for everything I had done for you for thirty years. People looked at me and smiled, and clapped. For a brief time, I was yours, I was your BB and I was loved.

But when I walked up to kiss you after the speech, you turned your back on me. I could feel your determination not to turn around and look at me. You were punishing me for organizing the party. I was doing what I thought would make you happy and you were treating me like an unwelcome guest. You didn't look at me again that night. Your speech had only been for show and I was gutted with disappointment.

Immediately after the formalities, Henry drove your parents and Amanda home. They were tired and the party was noisy. You hardly spoke to them because you were busy entertaining and impressing your friends and colleagues, so I invited them for lunch the next day. I could feel Sam's eyes on me as I went through the rooms offering birthday cake to guests. He spent some time watching me before he approached. He took the tray from me and put it down. "Come talk with me," he said. He took my hand and led me towards a couch. "I don't like to see you working so hard. Relax and let someone else do it. That's what kids are for."

I was grateful that he noticed. I was glad that someone had. Sam and I talked for a while about his children by his first and second wives and about our children. Then Sam looked at me as though he had something to tell me. He hesitated and then appeared to change his mind. I knew what he was going to say and I didn't want him to say it. I wanted to get away from him as quickly as possible. I was saved by Eleanor who came looking for me. I left Sam, but not before he gave my hand a squeeze and said, "If you need somebody to talk to…" I smiled at him and moved away to take the tray back to the kitchen. I thought: *not in a hundred years.*

Later that night, when everyone had gone home, I sat amongst the debris of used glasses, uneaten cake, empty bottles and wrapping paper. You proclaimed yourself tired and went to bed. There would be no thanks for me in private. I sat there for a long while in the dark, thinking and sipping wine. Had the party been worth it? Had I worked so hard for nothing? Did having friends, family and colleagues at your party remind you of everything that you might lose? Would it help you decide to stay? I had my doubts.

I told you I didn't want a party, I hear you say. I know, I know. I reply. I thought you would change your mind when everyone came. I thought you would see how much effort I had put in and know how much I loved you. I thought you'd see how much we all loved you. *I didn't need the extra pressure,* I hear you say. *Things were already hard enough!* Hard enough? Was I making it harder? *Yes, much harder!* I hear you say. Good, I reply. You deserve it.

I was angry with you and with myself for being such a fool. I poured myself another glass of wine and sipped it slowly. I imagined myself leaving you. I knew Anne would say I should write a list of your positive aspects and what I would miss about you, but I didn't want to. I was angry and disappointed. I was hurting *so* much. I wanted to think about what I *wouldn't* miss about you. I got out my journal and pen. I turned on a lamp, curled up on the couch with my glass of wine and for the second time I wrote the kind of list that people write when they are hurting badly and need to vent.

Here is what I wrote:

What would I *not* miss about you? To start with, I wouldn't miss all those things that most women don't like about living with men. I wouldn't miss the whole toilet-seat-up-seat-down-your-aim-would-help thing, and how you leave one square of toilet paper on the cardboard roll just so you won't have to change it. It has never occurred to you to clean a toilet, change a nappy or make a bed, or to do anything that you consider beneath you, anything that you call 'women's work'. I wouldn't miss your refusal to learn to cook anything more substantial than a boiled egg or a barbecued sausage.

I wouldn't miss you believing that if you are sick, you are close to dying and need constant, sympathetic ministration, but if I am sick, I should still be able to get up and cook dinner. I wouldn't miss your persistent and unthinking assumption that if you happen to do anything around the house, it is because you are helping me, which always implies that it is really my job and that I am somehow inadequate because I didn't get it done myself. I remind you every Tuesday night to take out the rubbish bins. They've had to be taken out every Tuesday night for twenty-six years and yet you still need reminding. Why is that?

I wouldn't miss your assumption that it is my job to do all the laundry. My only victory in twenty-six years was your work shirts. You complained that I didn't iron them well enough so I made you iron them yourself.

I have to notice and congratulate you for *every* little thing you do in the house, even though I have done those things entirely unnoticed, for our entire married life. If I don't notice or heap praise on you, you sulk. If I point out that I have been doing it since forever, you accuse me of being snippy. If I do praise you, you strut around like a conquering hero and then you do nothing else for a long time. I definitely wouldn't miss that.

You always assume that if I am upset, I must be due for my period. It could never have anything to do with the fact that you are behaving like a chauvinistic jerk. I have to play my favorite music only in my car, or when you are not around. I have to turn off the radio the minute you come home so you can turn on the television to watch news and current affairs programs every night – every single night. *I need to stay informed*, I hear you say. But I don't want my life inundated with all that misery, I tell you again and again.

I wouldn't miss how you crunch quickly and noisily through your share of the chocolate while we watch television and then look resentfully and longingly at the chocolate I still have until I have to give you some. You drink milk or juice straight from the carton and what's worse, you put the empty cartons back in the fridge. You also put empty cereal boxes back in the cupboard. You put your used tea bags in the kitchen sink instead of the rubbish bin. *But I was draining them!* I hear you say. No, you weren't, you were leaving them there.

You can never find anything unless, or even if, it is right in front of your eyes. You call me to come from the other side of the house because you can't be bothered moving a few things to find what you are looking for. You complain about the size of print on newspapers, telephone books and menus because you won't admit that you now, like me, need reading glasses. I wouldn't miss your nail clippings in the bedroom carpet, your shaving remains in the bathroom sink, your short and curlies in the shower or your smelly socks under the bed.

When I ask you to fix something, you promise to do it but never get around to it. When I eventually ask Henry or get a handy man to do it, you complain that I haven't given you enough time to do it, even if it is weeks later. You say that you were getting around to doing it, that you were *just about to do it* when you see that it has been done, and you resent the cost of the lousy job the other person did.

I have to be the one to remember and do something about the birthdays of everyone in your family that you think needs a card or gift. I wouldn't miss being your social secretary and the finder of your missing ties, socks and keys. You assume that I will always be the one cooking Christmas dinner for your entire family. Every year, I do all the work, organizing and inviting, putting up the tree and decorations, ordering, preparing, present-buying, cooking and the cleaning up. You think you are the king of the world if you turn on the barbecue. There is so much that you take for granted.

I have to take into account your fussiness about food, every day and at every meal. I figure we have been married for twenty six years and if, for the sake of simplicity, we have had three hundred dinners together each year, it would mean we have had seven-thousand eight-hundred dinners together, most of which I prepared, and for all of which I had to take your fussiness into account. That's also a lot of dinners where I am not able to have what I might want.

If we stay together 'until death us do part' which, say, is another thirty years, and we still have dinner together three-hundred times a year (as you know, math is not my strong suit so I am keeping it simple), it would make a total of sixteen-thousand, eight-hundred dinners together over fifty-six years. That's not counting breakfasts and lunches on the weekends. Sixteen-thousand, eight-hundred dinners is a lot of dinners and I will have cooked almost all of them.

Sixteen-thousand, eight-hundred dinner conversations are also a lot of conversations! It's not surprising we often have little to say to each other at the dinner table. I used to look at married couples sitting in restaurants. They seldom spoke and if one did, it was to ask the other to pass the salt. I used to think it was romantic that they were so relaxed and comfortable in each other's company. It now occurs to me that they might have been bored.

There are so many restaurants we can't visit because they don't serve anything you are willing to eat. I'm talking about Indian, Lebanese, African, Japanese, Thai or Greek restaurants. I always cringe during your instructions to waiters about what you do and don't eat. I have to sit there listening to you telling someone else how limited you are in your choice of food – it can be chicken as long as it is the breast of the chicken, it can be beef as long as all the fat is cut off. It can be vegetables as long as they are peas, carrots and beans. I could go on, but why bother? You know what I mean.

I wouldn't miss, when I tell you I am thinking about doing a project, a class or a new course, the way you use bad news stories to point out why I couldn't possibly do it, stories about how hardly anybody else has been able to do it and even if they have, (and they must have been a lot smarter than me), their lives are miserable as a result. You can be discouraging and condescending.

When I tell you I have had a bad day, you come up with all the reasons why it is my fault and what I should do to fix it. You never understand that all I want is a hug, not a lecture.

I wouldn't miss how, on the rare occasions when you consent to take me to live theatre, when we are about to leave, you always find one last-minute thing to do and that thing nearly always makes us late. Then if we get there and the show has already started, and the usher won't let us in until immediately, you give him or her a hard time as though it is their fault we are late. I am embarrassed and the evening is spoiled. You also complain about the cost and inconvenience of going out, when an evening watching television would be much cheaper and easier.

Do you remember when we were going to take the train to friends in the country and you had one last-minute thing to do before we left? We arrived on the platform just as the train was leaving and you tried to open the doors to push me in. The guard told you off and you acted like a total jerk. He was trying to protect me and you snarled at him. Then we didn't get our ticket money back because the guard said it was our fault we were late. We had to take the tram all the way back home to get the car. Somehow, you managed to make me feel as though it was my fault even though I had warned you we would be late. We drove in almost total silence.

It is so hard for you to apologize about anything, big or small.

You refuse to ask for directions, no matter how lost we are. You insist you know where you are going and then we drive around in circles. You assume you should always have the best bits of the Sunday newspaper first. You say 'presumedly' when you mean presumably. You tell stories to people, over and over again, apparently without ever considering how many times I might have had to listen to them.

Overall, there are lots of things I wouldn't miss about you. This list is full of petty annoyances, the sort of things that should not matter when we talk about the love of our life. I have just never thought about them all at the same time before and they add up to a lot. It is a long list. It is a *very* long list.

I looked at what I had written and breathed a sigh. I also sat there thinking that if you ever gave up that dumb bimbo, things were going to have to change around here. You were going to have to lift your game because I was not going to put up with everything that I had put up with for years. I was going to make some changes. I would start with the issue of your parents' care. I would make it your responsibility. Now that you have so much (listen to the ironic tone here, Mike), *so much work* to do on the weekends, you can take care of your own parents on Wednesday mornings. Yes, I decided, if you stop seeing that cow and want to stay married to me, you will have to get used to lots of changes.

The future began to weigh heavily on me. I wrote: if I leave you now, I can have another thirty years of meals, thirty-two thousand, eight-hundred-and-fifty breakfasts, lunches and dinners with lots of other people in lots of other places. That's only until I reach the age of seventy-eight and I plan to live much longer than that.

Eventually, I wore myself out and went to bed. You were already snoring and I added that to the list of things I wouldn't miss. I sighed. I no longer felt angry. I was thinking about thirty-two thousand, eight-hundred-and-fifty meals and more, and where I might want to eat them. I toyed seriously, for the first time, with the idea of leaving you.

Your treatment of me on the day of your fiftieth birthday party was Strike One.

Chapter 12

Learning To Imagine

The next day I went to the bank to open a new account and arranged to have my pay transferred into it. If you were spending money on that woman, I was going to make damn sure it wouldn't be any of mine. I also went to a different bank and opened a secret savings account. If I was going to be on my own at any time in the future, I wanted to make sure I was ready for it. I started thinking about saving as much money as possible every week and putting it away where you couldn't reach it.

Anne looked tanned and relaxed when I saw her next on June 6. She'd had a great time in America. When she asked me how I was feeling, I told her I was not feeling so angry or vengeful anymore. I had been working hard at keeping you. I had made lots of lists: to-do lists, to-improve lists, to-invite lists, to-change lists. I had worked on all those lists. I told her about your birthday party and what a complete waste of time it was. I was getting tired and now that I was no longer angry, I was not sure what I felt. I was both frustrated and overwhelmed.

"They're feelings," said Anne. "One more step up the emotional ladder."

"You mean how I am feeling is a good thing?"

"I sure do."

I told Anne that nothing I had done had stopped you seeing your girlfriend. I was beginning to imagine that your leaving was inevitable and that I would live the rest of my life alone. I was imagining the worst. I was now sure I would end up an old, bitter ex-wife with no money, one who only hears from friends when they have been to visit you and your new wife in my old home and they want to rub in how well you are doing – what a lovely person the FC is, (really!), how your new baby is (just adorable), and what overseas trips (Tahiti this year!) you're taking that I can't afford to take.

"You worked hard to keep him and it left you frustrated and overwhelmed. Right?" said Anne.

I nodded.

"You were trying to change things by using action, but you weren't taking into account the atmosphere in your home that you were creating with that action."

I looked at her. I knew by now that if I waited, she would explain it in a way I would understand.

"You can't change things using action alone," said Anne. "It is like paddling upstream. You have to take into account the atmosphere, the feelings you are creating, because they are more powerful than any of the actions you take."

"I know *now*," I moaned. "I tried so hard and ended up exhausted and irritable. No wonder he didn't want to be home."

"So now you're imagining his leaving?" asked Anne.

"Yes," I replied sadly, "or I'm imagining leaving him. It's getting me down. Life with him is miserable but I am afraid that life without him would be so much worse."

"Well, given that you're just imagining it, why not imagine it the way you want it to be? You can choose to think about the 'what if' in a positive way."

"The 'what if'"?

"Yes," said Anne. "Don't you remember, when we first met, you had a list of 'what-if' questions a mile long? Now, aren't you saying, what if I'm poor, what if I'm lonely, what if I'm angry?"

"Yes all the time. It starts first thing every morning and dominates my day."

"What do you want?" she asked.

I thought, oh no, not this again, I get so tired of hearing this; it sounds like the chant of a demonstrating crowd.

"I want to be happy." I said irritably.

"So how about thinking, what if I'm happy? Try it."

"What if I'm happy," I said sullenly.

"How did that feel?" asked Anne.

"Like far-fetched nonsense."

"Is it more far-fetched than being poor, lonely and bitter?"

"They both feel a long way off in opposite directions, like two opposite ends of a long stick, but the negatives feel a bit closer."

"That's only because you've been practicing them longer. You have been saying those negative 'what-ifs' so long now that they feel automatic. It will take practice to turn them around, so start practicing now. Turn your attention to the positive end of that stick. Start with, what if I am happy?"

Reluctantly, I tried it. "What if I am happy, what if I have fun, what if I have money…" I gave up because it felt so false.

"But it feels so untrue," I complained.

"It doesn't matter that it's not true. All that negative stuff wasn't true either, but you kept thinking it. Keep going until you can feel a small breath of hopefulness."

"Okay, what if life gets better, what if I feel better; what if everything feels just a little better?" I stalled. I hadn't had enough practice with positive thoughts to get on a roll.

"That's a good start. Remember it doesn't have to be true, it is meant to help you feel hopeful."

"Hopeful?"

"Yes, that's the next step up your emotional ladder. So tell me what you can hope for."

"I can hope that he stops seeing her," I said sourly, knowing that this wasn't what Anne meant.

"This isn't about him. Make it about yourself."

"I can hope to get over this…"

"And be?" prompted Anne.

"Happy."

"How would you start getting happy? There's only one correct answer."

"Huh?" I stared at her.

"Think hopeful, happy thoughts. Catch your negative thoughts before they gather momentum. Stop them while they're small. Tweak them, and turn them around."

"It sounds like hard work."

"Harder than being miserable?" asked Anne.

"No, nothing could be harder than that."

"Start first thing in the morning when you wake up," she said. "Notice what you are thinking and set your intention to feel good. Choose to think about something hopeful. Start by finding one thing to appreciate. Focus on it for seventeen seconds and see what comes up."

"Why seventeen seconds?"

"It's a good number. When you're planning to do something, see it in your mind's eye going exactly the way you want it. Imagine everything going well."

"But will that get me what I want?" I asked.

"Yes, you will feel better."

"Is that all?"

"Isn't that enough?"

"Yes I suppose so. I know you have no magic solutions for changing Michael."

"That's because he is not here asking to be changed. *You* are," said Anne. "You see your happiness as tied up, locked in and dependent on him. How about making it tuned in, tapped in and turned on to who you are and what *you* want? Get happy. Practice happy thoughts. Do happy things. It will have the added benefit of making you easier to be around as well, and that could change everything."

I repeated silently Anne's words *'and that could change everything'*. Maybe if I relaxed, I would be nicer. Maybe if I were nicer, you might want to stay home. You might choose to be with me instead of your girlfriend. I promised Anne I would try.

"If you and I were meeting for lunch tomorrow," said Anne, "and I said I would *try* to be there by midday, how likely is it that I would be there on time?"

"Not very likely," I said. "You would be late."

"Then don't promise me you will try. Just do it," said Anne. "Now, tell me about your mother."

Another surprise question. My Mum gave birth to me when she was nearly forty years old, after years of trying, and she wasn't able to have any more children after me. She made a great effort not to spoil me or to smother me and allowed me to have as many friends over as I wanted, almost whenever I wanted. I think she liked having the extra children around. She made my home a haven and taught me so many things. She loved my Dad and after he died, she got on with her life. She never married again but had lots of friends and was always busy, until a sudden stroke took her away at the age of eighty-eight, almost six months ago.

"Tell me about how she died," Anne said gently.

"She was in her garden and had a stroke. Her neighbor found her unconscious, called an ambulance and then called me. The following day she recovered consciousness for a short while before having another stroke that killed her."

"So, she died doing something she enjoyed?"

"Yes, she loved her little garden," I sighed.

"No pain, suffering, long hospital stays, tubes up her nose, nursing homes, spoon-feeding, adult nappies, palliative care?"

"No, none of that," I replied.

"No dementia, not recognizing you and complaining to you that her daughter hasn't been to visit her for months?"

"No, none of that either." What was Anne was getting at?

"She died happily then, didn't she!" said Anne.

"Died happily?"

"I imagine that there is one thing you and your mother had in common," said Anne.

"And that was?"

"You both hoped she would die before you."

I hadn't thought about it like that before, but it was true. Mum wouldn't have coped if I had died before her. I think the grief would have killed her.

"So it was an easy death," Anne continued. "She died before you, while she was still sane and active, quickly, relatively painlessly and without extended stays in hospitals or nursing homes."

"That's a positive way of looking at it," I said. I felt, however, that Anne was saying I had no right to be sad.

"It's a helpful way of looking at it," said Anne. "People make the mistake of treating death as though it is not supposed to happen, as though it is some kind of failure or punishment, which of course it isn't. If we look at death as inevitable, we can accept it for what it is and then look for what is positive about it."

"So I can't be sad about her dying?" I asked.

"Of course you can if you want to, but does it help?"

"No, it doesn't. She was a lovely person, we had a great relationship and I miss her, and I can be glad that I got to hold her hand and have her smile at me before she died."

"Yes you did," said Anne. "That's a lot more than many people get. Tell me what she loved about you."

I sat for a few minutes, feeling a range of emotions, love, loss and appreciation. What did she love about me?

I smiled.

"She loved the simple fact that she was able to have a baby after so many years of waiting. She loved me because I was funny and helpful. We shared a wicked sense of humor. She loved me because I enjoyed her company."

"You should see the look on your face," said Anne. "It is an expression of love and joy. There's no need to grieve about her death. How about imagining that she is still here, that she is on your side and is hoping for good things for you?" She paused. "What would she advise you to do about Michael?"

"She would want me to do what makes me happy," I replied.

"Your mother is a smart woman," said Anne.

Chapter 13

Winter Of My Discontent

It was early July, cold, dark and wet. The sun rose late and set early. At the childcare center, almost every child had a snotty nose and every member of staff had a cough. We kept passing the germs around to each other because parents either wouldn't or couldn't keep their sick children at home, even when they knew they were sick. It was frustrating and there wasn't much we could do about it. I was pessimistic and tired and the staff left me well alone. I couldn't find any dandelions to put in a glass, at work or at home and that made me more miserable.

When we were all grumpy, things went wrong. Staff called in sick, cars wouldn't start, meals got burned, the roof leaked, it rained constantly so we couldn't go outside, children squabbled with each other and cried for their mothers. At the end of the day, everyone was glad to see the back of everyone else. I cut myself preparing vegetables, I walked into the tow-ball on your car, I forgot to fill my car with petrol and it stopped in busy traffic. The front right tire hit a deep pot-hole and had to be replaced before it blew out. Something important I was supposed to do at work didn't get done and my staff were upset with me. I was beginning to understand some of Anne's words. The bad mood set a negative momentum. It felt like we were all thinking negative thoughts, which contributed to negative things happening.

Everything was going wrong and I couldn't tell you about it because so often, I didn't know where you were. You were working more on weekends. You said that work was so busy this year we couldn't take our usual trip up north. I was still worried that nothing would change. I wasn't waiting each night for you to come home and tell me you were leaving me, but I wasn't yet in a place where I could decide to do something for myself. Anne was right. My happiness seemed tied up, locked in and dependent on you. It didn't feel good at all.

I kept writing in my journal and looking for things to be hopeful about but they were thin on the ground. I tried imagining that things would turn out the way I wanted, but my mind sabotaged me at nearly every turn, so I listened repeatedly to the recordings of my sessions with Anne. 'Look for things to appreciate', she said. 'Imagine it the way you want it', she said. 'Relax and get happy, and that could change everything', she said. I no longer watched crime or drama on television, I didn't listen to miserable songs on the radio and I avoided the complainers amongst my friends and colleagues. I was tuned to the A. H. station and I practiced what I was being taught. I also went back to the DVD store and borrowed movies about women making choices and changes: 'Eat, Pray, Love', 'Moonstruck', 'The Holiday', 'Another Woman' and 'Home Before Dark'.

I borrowed lots of other movies to keep me occupied when you weren't home, many of which you would have refused to watch because they were chick flicks or had no macho violence in them.

I began to find some advantages in your not being at home. If you were not there, I didn't have to cook your dinner. I didn't have to cook at all. In fact, I could just stand at the kitchen sink and eat cold baked beans from a tin. That seemed to represent my mood. I was cold, tired and disappointed. I began to think I hated you more than I loved you. It wasn't much more, but I could feel the balance tipping. Nothing I tried had worked so I stood alone in the kitchen eating cold baked beans.

Not long after, it was my forty-eighth birthday. You forgot this year for the first time, and when I reminded you, you told me you would be away. I asked you to change your plans because your parents, the kids and our best friends were coming for dinner. It had been arranged weeks before. I could see you struggling to decide whether you would still go away, or whether you would have the inevitable argument with the FC about putting me first. In the end, you were there for my birthday, but it was a hollow victory for me because your mood was sour.

The present you gave me was thoughtless and impersonal; it was one of those powder/bath-salt packets that are given to elderly female relatives. When you saw it, you looked ashamed. The FC must have bought it and wrapped it. How she must have loved finding the most hideous old-lady present she could find! I put it straight into the Salvos bag.

Strike two.

Oh, my God, why didn't you say anything? I hear you ask. *If you had, maybe I wouldn't be in this mess!* Mess? I ask. *Yes, mess! She wants to live with me. She's made hints about having babies and for God's sake, I am fifty! You could have stopped it!* Hey, wait a minute! How is this suddenly my fault? You chose to have an affair! How could I have stopped it? When could I have stopped it? I don't know when it began! Would you have stopped it if I'd asked you to? *Yes! No…no, probably not. She is wonderf….* Don't go there! I don't want to hear about her!

Then you'd understand! I hear you say. Oh come on! I understand, believe me, I do understand! It's such a cliché. Older man, younger woman, mid-life crisis, believe me, I get it! She made you feel like a conquering hero and you wanted to get into younger knickers. It's just nature's old trick of getting one more child out of you, which it couldn't get out of the older wife. There's nothing magical about her. She wipes her butt like I do; she has seven meters of shit-filled pipes inside her like every other woman on earth! Believe me, there is nothing special about her. She is just younger. Was it boring having a devoted wife? Did you need more of a challenge?

I give up! I hear you say. Good! I reply. You deserve each other. I hope you will be very happy together – not really. I hope you suffer. I hope you suffer a lot.

But I might have said I'm sorry, I might have promised not to see her again. I hear you say. But you don't understand, Mike. I was just as afraid of *that*.

I knew that if I confronted you, and you said you would stop seeing her, it would be awful between us. I know you're a good and honest man (deep down). This affair was important to you, important enough for you to lie to me every day, for months. If I had said something and you apologized and stopped seeing her, we would have to 'get over the affair' and we would both be miserable. We might even have to get counselling and expose your love for another woman to a stranger, which would be humiliating for both of us. Even though you were the one having the affair, I would feel guilty, I would feel like the bad guy and I didn't want to be the bad guy.

Maybe, just maybe, you were with that woman because you loved her. If so, I would make you feel simultaneously like a stupid man in a mid-life crisis and a naughty little boy who'd been caught doing something nasty. I didn't want to do that to you, so it is possible I said nothing because I loved you. Maybe another reason was that I was beginning to think that I might not be up to the effort it would take to repair our relationship.

Remember Simon and Christine Anderson, our good friends who 'got over the affair'? All I remember about them was the pain in their eyes and their accusing and guilty glances at each other. They walked on egg shells, like wary strangers, for months. Christine could neither trust nor forgive. I didn't want that for us. Simon fell in love with a younger woman, a widow with two small children who sold him his coffee every morning on his way to work. They got chatting and he couldn't keep away from her. He loved the way she looked at his mouth when he spoke. She hooked him with her big breasts, her vulnerability and her unspoken promise of grateful sex.

Christine was a lost and desperate being. She raged and cried endlessly. She said bitterly, "That's what you get when you put all your eggs in one bastard!" She lost herself at the poker machines. She spent hours there nearly every day. She explained to me that when she sat in front of those machines, she could forget who she was; she didn't have to think about Simon or about anything at all.

One day she forgot to pick up their children from school and the principal called Simon. Christine had been at the poker machines and had lost track of time. Her gambling added to her problems and gave Simon another reason to criticize her. They went to counselling and he talked to you about it on your fishing trips, then you told me, but I couldn't tell her what he'd said.

Then they disappeared. They didn't return our calls or emails, probably because we knew too many of their secrets and seeing us was a sad reminder of that time in their lives. To this day, I don't know if they are still together or divorced.

I used to be afraid of the words divorce, divorced and divorcee. If we split up, I knew I would have to tick the 'divorced' box on application forms, forever. I would have to describe myself as a divorcee. I hated the idea of people describing me as 'newly divorced', which would make me sound needy, inadequate, a loser, an easy target because I wasn't 'getting any', or a complete bitch.

I was being asked to choose between being unhappily married or divorced, and back then, it wasn't an easy choice.

But the time was coming that a choice would have to be made. I had put my boat into a fast-moving steam and paddled hard against the current. I was paddling so hard, but getting nowhere and becoming more and more tired and defeated. I had, in fact, made everything worse and now I was exhausted from the effort. Being happy seemed like an impossible dream.

I began to feel my momentum slowing down. I stopped struggling against the current. I stopped trying so hard. Then I stopped trying altogether. I sat still in the boat and allowed the current to turn it and to carry me, to take me with it. I lay back and I breathed. I dropped the oars and let the current take my boat downstream.

Chapter 14

Dropping The Oars

It was July 20. I was so tired I couldn't get out of bed. I felt like a cicada shell left on a tree. The cicada spends years underground before making its long, arduous journey up a tree and climbs out of its own dried skin. The discarded shell clings to the bark of the tree even though the cicada itself has flown away. Nobody cares about the shell. Its usefulness is over. It just sits there until it falls apart or falls off.

I woke up alone, exhausted, so I lay very still, which gave me some relief. It was good not to have to jump up straight away, and get things done. I knew I was run down both physically and emotionally. It was unbearable to think that no matter what I had done, you wanted the FC more, that no matter how hard I had tried, you still chose her. I could barely face the day. I didn't want to get up. I didn't want to have to think or to pretend that everything was okay. I wanted to curl up somewhere and slip into unconsciousness. I missed you. I missed us. I missed your wink, your smile, your kiss on my neck and your pat on my butt as I stood at the kitchen sink.

It was seven months since Mum's death and it still felt like yesterday. It was five months since I had seen you with your girlfriend and that felt like yesterday as well. I lay there thinking about the day my Mum's neighbor telephoned, saying he had found her lying unconscious in her garden. Then, when she died the next day, I couldn't breathe, I couldn't take it in. The funeral was terrible. While we know that our parents are likely to die before we do, it is still devastating when it happens. Even now, I still expect to be able to go around to Mum's place and see her, hear her and feel her hug. I lay in bed thinking about my Mum and then I did as Anne suggested. I thought about what Mum and I loved about each other. I thought about how she had been able to avoid all the hardships of fragile old age. I found something to appreciate in it all.

I wanted the day to myself so I rang work and told them I wouldn't be in. I slowly got dressed and then drove myself down to the beach where I took a long walk and watched the horizon, and I called Anne.

I saw her two days later. Anne looked at me and knew it was over. She knew I had let go.

"I feel so stupid," I sighed.

"You're never stupid. Ever. You're always doing the best you can from where you are."

"I did everything I could think of."

"And how did that work out for you?" she asked. I smiled sadly and admitted that everything I had done for the past five months had been a dismal failure.

"I want to go to sleep, I want to hide. I want to run away." I sighed again.

"Where to?"

"I don't know. Anywhere, away from here."

"What would have to happen for you to feel better?" asked Anne.

"That's just it. I don't know. I just want to quit, to sleep, to stop."

"So stop. What would happen?"

"I don't know," I whispered.

"I mean, stop thinking that you can stop change when it's obvious that the momentum of change is already well on its way."

"You mean, just let the FC take him from me?"

"He's not your doll. If he goes, it is because *he* has decided to go. And stop blaming the other woman."

Anne sat back and looked sternly at me.

"And it's about time you stopped calling that woman the FC. It only holds you in a hateful holding pattern. Let it go."

What Anne said hurt. I sat there, feeling criticized. It had been easy blaming the FC. I had been doing it for months. She was so much easier to hate because I had never loved her, but hating her had stopped me thinking directly about you. If I stopped blaming her, I would have to focus on you. I would have to acknowledge that you were the one lying to me; you were the one cheating on me. You were deciding to spend long periods of time with another woman. You preferred to be with her and that hurt so much I didn't want to think about it, so I focused on her. Now I was being told I had to stop hating her. I had to focus on you and see you more clearly.

"You spent so much time in frenzied activity, trying to keep your husband away from his girlfriend, you didn't stop to think," said Anne. "Now, I want you to stop. I want you to think, to relax and enjoy what you can enjoy. I want you to find hopefulness, optimism and appreciation. There is no happy ending to an unhappy journey."

I wanted to argue with her. We had discussed this before. She had told me to get happy and think about something else, but I couldn't accept that everything I had done had been a complete failure. I felt criticized and small, so I got angry.

"Well," I retorted, "What about that woman whose son was killed by a drunk driver, and she started a group called MADD (Mothers against

Drunk Driving, in case you didn't know, Mike) and they got lots of road rules and laws changed in America. She got angry. She got things done!"

"Yes," said Anne, "but while she was just angry she couldn't do anything. When she mixed anger with the *hope* that she could make a difference to others, she was inspired to action. The catalyst was hopefulness."

"So all I have to do is be hopeful?" I snorted. "Like that will change anything!"

"Yes it will, but it needs to be general hope about feeling better, not hope that your husband dumps his girlfriend. It needs to be about you personally. All your efforts have been directed at keeping the status quo of your marriage, but they have driven him further away. How about letting go, just to see what happens? What if you are happy regardless of what he does?"

I gave her a hostile glance and said, "Yeah, right."

"No, I mean it. You can be, do and have whatever you want, but if your ultimate goal is to be happy and your happiness is tied to *his* behavior changing, you are at his mercy. The only way you can be happy is to loosen that knot."

"But how can I be happy without him?" I looked at her, defying her to give me an answer.

"Ah, a question we can work with. You tell me – how can you be happy *with or without* him?"

"I can't."

"Yes you can. You have done it before. I've seen it. Now, do it again."

I remembered our first session and replied "I can make lists of the positive aspects of what else is going on in my life like I did at the beginning."

"Back then," Anne said, "I distracted you at a time when you were totally unable to take any kind of action. Now I want you to focus *not only* on what is going well, but also on what *could* go well, on 'what if'. I want you to start thinking thoughts like 'what if', and 'wouldn't it be nice if…I want you to start imagining positive possibilities."

I sat there and looked at her. I repeated her words, "What if I could be happy with or without him?"

I felt nothing. Once again we were just playing with words and they didn't change a thing.

"The way I see it," said Anne, "you have choices." She got an A3 sheet of paper and a pencil from the cupboard. She put the paper down in front of me and drew lines, dividing the paper into six and writing as she spoke. "You can either continue as you are and be miserable (top left) or you can continue as you are and be happy (bottom left), you can make him or let him leave you and be miserable (middle top) or you can make him or let him leave you and be happy (underneath). You can leave him and be miserable (top right) or you can leave him and be happy (bottom right)."

Anne turned the sheet around to face me. Suddenly we were no longer just playing with words. She gave me the pencil and said, "Cross out the ones you definitely can't do. Just eliminate them."

I put a line through 'Continue as you are and be miserable', 'Make him or let him leave you and be miserable' and 'Leave him and be miserable'. I did not want to be miserable anymore. I was so tired of it, I would have done almost anything to end it.

"Now notice that you have three options left," said Anne. "Stay and be happy, make him or let him leave you and be happy, or leave him and be happy. Your choices are getting a little clearer. Can you eliminate another one on that page?"

I looked at her, looked down at the paper and back at her. It was too hard. It was frightening.

"Eliminate the one you have the least control over," said Anne.

I breathed deeply and crossed out the one where you leave me. I had no control over that. I couldn't let you leave or make you leave. I finally got that, but I couldn't leave you either because that would mean leaving my home. I kept that thought to myself because I knew what Anne would say. There was also another, unspoken option. I could talk to you, but even then, I still wasn't ready to do that.

"Now," said Anne, "I want you to choose the option that gives you a feeling of relief. You are not looking for great joy here, just a feeling of relief. Focus on the one that gives you a sense of relief and look for the positive aspects of it. The rest you can figure out as you go along."

"I can stay and be happy. I can leave him and be happy." I repeated each sentence two or three times and slowed them down. There were surges of conflicting feelings within me. I was confused and scared. The options were clear but I was not yet ready to choose.

"Staying and being happy will mean you have some work to do in your relationship with Michael," said Anne. "It will mean repairing old pipes. It will mean working on the relationship. It might mean couples' counselling. Leaving Michael will mean laying new pipes. If you can't make up your mind, spend a day pretending you have decided to stay and see how you feel at the end of the day. Speak and think as though the decision has been made. Then spend the following day doing the opposite and see how you feel at the end of it. The final decision will be easier to make if you've practiced both options."

I didn't understand the new metaphor about pipes but what Anne said made sense. I took the sheet home with me.

The next day, I pretended that I was going to stay with you and be happy anyway. By the end of the day, I was tired and depressed. I was standing alone in the kitchen eating leftovers when it occurred to me that I could be eating asparagus dipped in garlic aioli. I remembered Anne's suggestion that I make a list of 'what if I could be happy without you' scenarios. I started to think about positive possibilities to see if I could get on a roll. I got out my journal and started with the asparagus.

What if I can eat asparagus...and onions...and garlic...and raw salmon... and eggplant...and coriander?

What if I can eat Indian, Thai, Greek, African or Lebanese food?

What if I can eat whatever and whenever I like?

What if things are good? What if I have fun?

What if I can go out to the ballet and concerts and galleries and the beach? What if I am happy? What if I leave you? What if I insist you leave me? What if I never regret losing you? What if it was the best thing I ever did? What if I have an exciting new life with new friends and new lovers?

What if I meet a great man who suits my new life?

What if life is interesting and adventurous and fun?

I wrote for over an hour.

The following day, I pretended I was ending the relationship with you. I spoke to myself about all the things I could do without you. By the end of the day, I felt quietly exhilarated. The way was clearer and yet it was another month before I accepted that my best option was to end the relationship with you and be happy.

I finally started work on a list of your positive aspects. Anne had suggested such a list months before but I hadn't been able to do it. I began to look for things about you that would get me started. It wasn't hard. There were so many things that made you dear to me.

I thought about what it was I have always loved about you, and as days passed, I added to the list. I became more mellow around you. You responded to that by being home, just a little earlier and just a little bit more often. You began to look me in the eye, but now, I was avoiding your gaze. Now I was the one with a secret. I was thinking of getting rid of you.

I saw Anne again two weeks later.

"Still overwhelmed?" she asked.

"Not so much. I've started looking at the positive end of the stick."

"Tell me about something that used to frustrate you, but doesn't now."

"You mean about my husband?"

"No, definitely not. Choose something simple and unrelated."

I sat and thought. "The tight lids of jars, I would twist them, beat them, heat them, whack them on the bench and then, in frustration I would wait till Michael got home."

"How did you feel?"

"Helpless and annoyed."

"How did you solve it?"

"Henry showed me that if I put the handle of a teaspoon under the cap and twisted it, I could break the air seal and the lid would come off easily."

"So he taught you to do something different. Now, it is time to do something different."

"I don't get you."

"Do you still want to keep Michael?"

"Yes and no," I replied. "I've done everything I can to get him to stop seeing his girlfriend and nothing's worked. I've done everything except confront him."

"You've twisted the cap, you've whacked it on the kitchen bench, you've held it under the hot water tap, but it won't budge, right?"

"I like the metaphor. I would like to do all that to him." I smiled.

"I'm sure you would," said Anne, "but it's time to do something else. Remember, it goes: thought first, feeling second, action third. So tell me your thoughts."

"They go like – I am beginning to discover things I would like to do but can't. I am stuck here with him and his affair but I don't know what I would do with the rest of my life if I left."

"You still can't talk to him?"

"No. I am so afraid I would fall apart and that he would take advantage of that, and I would have to leave. Things are a little better between us, but there is a huge elephant in the room that we can't talk about, so I doubt we could ever again be truly relaxed and happy together."

"Tell me what you want," said Anne.

I sighed. "I wrote a list of all the things I could do without him and it has got me so excited and so unsettled, but it still feels a long way off."

"You're going to be all right soon, I know," said Anne. "From your perspective, feeling okay seems a long way off, but it won't be long before you get your power back and you can make good choices. I know you think that's a massive stretch but one thing I know for sure is, you will get there, because you have come so far already."

I felt reassured by Anne's confidence in me. It lifted me a little out of my gloom.

"Let me tell you a little story that might help," said Anne. "My mother had a brain tumor which was operated on when she was your age. The surgeon told her that because of the size and position of the tumor, she may be left blind or 'retarded' by the surgery." Anne noticed my eyebrows lift. "Retarded was an acceptable word at that time… He told my mother she had to have the surgery anyway to stop the damage being done by her frequent grand mal seizures, so she agreed. When she woke up from the operation, she lay there for a long time, too terrified to open her eyes. She was afraid she would be blind. Slowly, she opened one eye and she could see. 'God!' she yelled. 'I'm retarded! I'm retarded!' The nurses came running.

"The thought of being intellectually disabled haunted her. She didn't feel any different, but she worried when she went from one room to another and forgot what she went there for, which you and I know is quite normal. She worried if she forgot people's names, which is also normal. She couldn't stand feeling so unsure of her own mental ability, so she enrolled at Melbourne University at the age of fifty and completed an Arts degree with Honors. She sent a copy of her degree to the surgeon, assuring him that she was neither blind nor 'retarded'. She got her power back."

"That's a great story and your mother sounds like an amazing woman," I said. "But how can I get my power back? I am bored with what I am doing. I am feeling old and as far as I can see, I have no particular skills or talents. I'm not academic or sporty. I'm not artistic or creative. I failed Art at high school because I couldn't see the point of it. I could never learn to read music; it was all just sparrows on power lines to me, so I can't play an instrument. I can't do anything. I don't even have a disability, disease or brain tumor to overcome. I'm too old and it's all too late. I need to do something different but I just don't know what, and I feel like I've run out of time."

"Look at me," said Anne fiercely. "Do I look too old to you? Am I too old to do anything of value?"

"No, of course not," I replied, suddenly embarrassed.

"Then neither are you. Your only disability is your negative attitude. You are forty-eight and I am fifty-six, which means you will be my age in 2020. You will be your mother's age in 2052. That's a long way off. You have at least forty years ahead of you, all being well. You can do whatever you want. Your only problem now is that you have no idea what you want to do. You keep arguing for your limitations. You keep telling me what you can't do. Now, tell me what you can do!"

Nothing came to mind. I was good at my work; I was enthusiastic about the good care of children, but that was about it.

"When you have stopped arguing for your limitations," she said, "new ideas will come, but you need to let go of thinking that you can't do anything. I am talking about becoming more of who you really are – intelligent, energetic, relaxed and nice to be around. I have some homework for you." She passed me a small thin book called 'Illusions' by Richard Bach. "Read this. Don't analyze it, don't over-think it, just read it and bring it to the next session."

Then Anne asked me, "What would you have to think about, in order to be happy?"

"I would have to think about my work, my children, my…" My mind went dry. Those things weren't enough; they didn't fill the void anymore. I sat there unable to speak.

Anne looked expectantly at me.

"I would have to think about *new* things, new ideas or new projects," I said.

Anne nodded. "You would also have to see yourself in a new light. What would that new light have to be?"

"I would have to be able to see myself as capable of change and of accomplishing something new."

"Yes, that's right. Thinking of yourself as 'just a wife' has kept you paddling upstream just so you could stay in the same place. Now you are ready to go with the stream, to consider new possibilities."

"You mean just float? That just sounds lazy. Shouldn't I keep working hard?"

"How has that worked out so far?"

"Yeah, yeah, I get it, but I can't sit around and do *nothing*."

"You wouldn't be doing *nothing* for long. Is keeping your husband still your ultimate goal?"

"No," I admitted. "It's to be happy, whether we are together or not."

"If you relax and do nothing for a little while," said Anne, "you will be inspired to action, not motivated as you have been."

"What's the difference?"

"Motivation is about pushing yourself to achieve a goal. Inspiration is when ideas come to you. Inspiration is as simple as floating downstream. Here is some more homework for you. I want you to become aware of how often you use the word *should*."

"Why shouldn't I?" I joked.

"Because *should* is a word that implies conflict and judgment. There is a silent 'but' at the end of every sentence, like, I should walk around the block every morning…"

I could feel the silent 'but' there. I tried a few sentences for myself and realized that the word *should* made me feel resentful and guilty and a little hurt. I should be more attractive, I should go to the gym, I should be able to make you love me and I should be able to keep you. I felt inadequate.

"Be particularly aware of when other people tell you what *they* think you *should* do," said Anne. "They are only telling you what *they* want you to do, and it usually has nothing to do with what *you* want. It is their perspective, not yours. Put an elastic band on your wrist and tweak it gently every time you say should, and then swap it for could, or want or would like to."

"Should I also do it for the words must, or have to, or ought to, or supposed to or obliged to?" I smiled.

Anne looked at me with amusement.

"You are going to do a lot of tweaking in the first week, I think," she said. She sat back and smiled too. "It will be interesting to see what you do next."

I laughed. That was such a light-hearted, unexpected perspective. She was right. I could stop the effort and the worrying and just watch what I did next. It was time to think even more seriously about leaving you, but I was not quite ready yet. I had to think first about how I could keep my home.

I read 'Illusions' three times. It was intriguing and puzzling. It was about a mechanic who became a messiah and then quit, and it was about flying airplanes and selling joy rides across the American mid-west with a miracle man. But it was a book I really needed to read. I could feel something shifting in me at an unconscious level. It was like waves in an underground lake, caused by earth tremors, if such a thing is possible. Nothing on the surface changed but deep down, I did.

I began to understand that it doesn't matter what anyone else thinks. It only matters what I think and I can think whatever I like.

Chapter 15

Floating

For the next few weeks, I relaxed more at work and at home. I didn't organize any dinners except for Eleanor and Henry. I hired a cleaner to do the housework. I used some of the money I had saved for our holiday and gave myself a holiday from cleaning. It was such a relief. I had more time for myself and I used it to write more in my journal. I wrote about the events of the last six months. Then I listened to the recordings of my sessions with Anne and transcribed some of them into the journal.

The rest of my holiday savings went into my secret bank account. I walked and cycled, I read more, swam at the pool and joined an aqua exercise class, which was fun. Most of the women in the class were older than me, some by a long way, and their energy, discipline and enthusiasm amazed me. They invited me to join them at a coffee shop after the class. I had delightful conversations with them. Most of the women were retired, yet they were busier than they had been when they were younger. They had plans and projects, worked part time, took classes, looked after grandchildren and great grandchildren. They volunteered in the community for libraries, hospitals and meals on wheels, and they served on committees. Three of them were writing a play together. They were a very impressive group of women, so I made room in my schedule for both the aqua class and the coffee afterwards. There was a lot I could learn from those women.

I played with the children at work, and talked at length with their parents. I began to pay more attention to their concerns and started looking for answers. When you went away, I thought about going away too. I thought about doing things that had nothing to do with you. I took myself out to dinner occasionally and went to restaurants I couldn't go to with you. One of my favorites was a Japanese restaurant where I could eat raw salmon sashimi. I learned to be comfortable by myself and not resort to reading, writing or playing Sudoku on my iPad. It took a while.

It became much more fun than eating out with you. I used to feel sorry for people who ate alone, but now I was one of them and I didn't feel sorry for myself at all. I looked on eating alone in restaurants as character-building. Besides, the food was delicious and I was starting to get my figure and my energy back.

At work, I delegated more. My assistant and I discussed the possibility of her taking on a more senior role, and she was pleased. She had been bored and wanted to do something with more responsibility. Then it occurred to me that *I* was bored. I was bored with my life, my work and bored with you. There was no better word for it than that. I had stopped the momentum of trying to make something happen, and now I seemed to be just floating. I had stopped putting all my effort into angry, vengeful thoughts and insane frenetic activity, and now I was utterly bored. With Anne's help, I had dragged myself up from the rungs of despair, helplessness, grief, rage, revenge, anger, frustration and overwhelm. I felt like I was now sitting square in the middle of the ladder in boredom, just one rung above pessimism, and looking up toward optimism, enthusiasm and passion.

Initially, the boredom scared me. I thought my life was going to simply fade away into nothing. I thought I would have to do the same things over and over until the day I died. I didn't know what else I could do. I was still married to you, so I didn't think there were any new or interesting options, but I was encouraged by Anne's confidence in me. I practiced what she had suggested, and continued to write my lists.

I started to dream, and each dream started with the words 'What if' and 'Wouldn't it be nice if…won't it be nice when…

I learned to enjoy sleeping alone in our bed. I stopped arranging your pillows lengthways down the middle of the bed to pretend you were there. In fact, I threw your pillows off the bed and moved mine to the middle. I sang Kelly Clarkson's song, 'Stronger'. Occasionally, I reached across to your side and was startled when I touched cold sheets. Then I remembered you were somewhere else with someone else, but I didn't cry about it anymore. It was what it was, and it was making me stronger.

On the nights you were there, I found myself beginning to resent the space you took up in the bed. You had begun to show interest in having sex with me again and I wasn't sure I wanted that. My heart just wasn't in it. I resented your snoring, I resented your farts and I resented you elbowing me when I snored. I looked at your sleeping face and saw only a stranger.

I began to wish you weren't there and I thought long and hard about leaving. I almost hoped you would come home and make the decision for me, by telling me you had decided to leave me. Then it would be your fault and I would be perfectly justified in kicking you out. That way I could keep my home. How strange it was that I had begun to want something I had previously been dreading.

On Saturdays when you were not home, I woke up whenever I felt like it. I lay still for a while and asked myself what I would like to think about and I set my intention to feel good. The cheerful Spring weather made it easier for me. It was as though the days themselves had decided to start in a good mood.

I sang, hummed and whistled, and by mid-morning, the housework and laundry were done. What did we do all weekend? There had always been so much on our list: lawns, weeds, gutters and cleaning. Did we ever ask ourselves whether we wanted to do any of it? Were we in such a rut after the kids left home that we did it all without thinking? Imagine that. We were living our lives without thinking. Maybe we kept busy to avoid the moment when there was nothing left to do and we would have to face each other and say, "Now what?"

One Monday morning, while you were faffing around with your briefcase, slurping your coffee and crunching your cereal, I was thinking, for God's sake just go! Then I thought, wait a minute, did I just think that? Do I want you out of here? Yes, I do, but what does that mean? I stood at the sink, breathing and looking at the kitchen clock. I repeated the thought for seventeen seconds; I can't wait for you to go. Then another thought followed it; I can do *whatever I want* when you aren't here. I can do *whatever I want.* Seventeen seconds later, another thought followed. I can *only* do what I want when you aren't here, and life would be more enjoyable if you weren't here. In fact, life would be more enjoyable if I weren't here either. My heart began to beat faster. I needed to move away from you and breathe, so I went out to the garden and spent some time looking for a dandelion.

There, deep in the corner of the garden, I found the first dandelion flower I had seen for a while. I put it in a vase on the windowsill where it looked at me through its round, beautiful, golden face. It reflected the sun perfectly. Every time I walked past it on the windowsill, I smiled. I was getting my power back and maybe, finally, I would be able to talk to you.

That night I looked at the dandelion, took a deep breath and asked you what was going on. You apologized to me for the past six months, and then on the spur of the moment, I decided to put you to the test by asking you if you were seeing someone else. I thought if you told me the truth, I might be able to stay. But I could no longer pretend that you hadn't lied to me every day. I couldn't pretend it had never happened. I wanted and needed honesty from you. I needed the elephant in the room to go away.

"What happened over the past six months?" I asked. "You just disappeared. You were like a stranger."

"I know," you said. "I'm sorry, but work was so incredibly busy. The inner-city residential market is so competitive and cut-throat and I had to be right on top of my game. There was always a meeting, a conference, a tax audit, an urgent case or a difficult client."

"You were always away from home," I whispered, and then I took a deep breath. "I thought there was someone else."

You looked at me with a fleeting expression of alarm and then went on about contracts that had to be done and deals that had taken all of your time. You were not going to tell me the truth. That woman was going to be the elephant in the room for the rest of our lives. Things were improving between us and you had been around a little more often, but because you could not be honest with me, it would never be good enough. It was then that I knew I didn't want to live with you anymore.

I wanted to say Strike Three but there was a small corner of wistful hope that somehow, some day, something could be repaired and renewed. It was a very small corner but it was still there. In another corner were my new dreams where I was planning to get you out of my life, when I had done the last thing I still needed to do.

I saw Anne next on August 6 and she asked me where I was on the emotional ladder. I admitted that I was bored and that I wasn't sure I wanted to stay married to you. I didn't know if I wanted to continue this life.

"Are you suicidal?" asked Anne.

"No, no, I don't mean I want to die or anything. I've just had enough of *this* life. I've had enough of this husband, this job, this set of friends, this life in general, and I am bored. I feel like my life's a movie and I've left the cinema half way through. I don't want to go back into the cinema but I don't know what I am supposed to do next."

"Remember, there is no should; there is no supposed to and there is no must, no ought to and no have to. There is only want. What do you want to do now?"

"Part of me wants to leave him and be happy. I want to be in a different movie with a different life."

"What sort of movie do you want it to be? Would it be a tragedy, horror, science fiction, romantic comedy? How about 'How Stella Got Her Groove Back'?" Anne smiled.

I laughed and asked, "Those are my options? Eat, Pray, Love? Under the Tuscan Sun? Belonging? I don't think so. I can't see myself plotting revenge or in an Ashram in India and I certainly won't be inviting my husband and his girlfriend over for afternoon tea."

"What would have to be different for you to be interested in your life?" Anne asked.

"Well, I would have to do something else or be somewhere else."

"That sounds like a quantum leap and a bit like a movie, but quantum leaps seldom work in real life. Small, logical steps work better. What is the first, small, logical thing you could do to relieve the boredom?"

"I could take a holiday," I replied thoughtfully. "I have long service leave coming up at the end of the year so I could do something or go somewhere. I want to be happy but I don't think I want to travel overseas to find myself, or find a younger or better lover, although that doesn't sound so bad."

Anne understood that I was not being serious. She told me that it is only when the brain is bored that it can make room for new ideas.

"What does happiness look like to you now?" she asked.

"I don't know."

"Just as an experiment, I would like you to imagine that there is a higher being that knows who you are and what you want."

"You mean like God? Are you getting religious on me?" I was astonished.

"Heaven forbid, no!" exclaimed Anne. "But we have never discussed your beliefs. Are they relevant to this situation?"

"Not really," I said. "I believe in a Universal force with no favorites. I always have."

"Not God?"

"No, the word 'god' is too loaded for me. God is a being who entitles himself to say that he loves us while he threatens us with eternal hell-fire if we don't belong to the right club, and it's based on something written by men thousands of years ago for nomadic desert tribes who thought the world was flat."

"Club?"

"You know, church, synagogue, mosque, temple."

"So, you prefer the word Universe?"

"Or Source," I said. "I think all of humanity comes from the one source and that our bodies, our beliefs and laws have evolved through time, climate and geography. I don't know if it was all done by a god. I do think there must be someone or something higher than us because mankind isn't clever enough to scrape enough dirt together to make this planet, or to keep it in orbit in perfect proximity to the sun and other planets. I don't make my own nails grow and I can't make seeds sprout. Something does but I don't know what that is. Why do you ask?"

"To see what we can use to get you moving in the direction of what you want." said Anne. "Some people feel more confident with the idea of having angels or other religious figures on their side. Some people like the idea that there is a higher self that knows why we were born, has a plan for us and loves us unconditionally."

"That would be nice. It would be comforting to believe in something that loves us unconditionally," I replied wistfully. "I want to be happy, simply happy and safe."

"Safe?" asked Anne. "You've mentioned that word before. What does 'safe' mean to you?"

"Like money in the bank, home, friends and family."

"Hmm, safe, you want to have safety, do you?" Anne looked skeptical. "What about having clarity, abundance, eagerness, passion, purpose, love, decisiveness and appreciation. What about being adventurous, determined, excited, daring, exhilarated, expansive, delighted, joyful and free?"

"Wow!" I laughed. "They are some amazing words!"

I loved the sound of all those words. They were words I had never used to describe myself or my life. They sounded simultaneously thrilling and impossible.

"Tell me," said Anne, "what is one small thing that you could do to make a difference in your life?"

"I could go out a little more and see the things I want to see."

"What would stop you doing that?"

I explained that I had started taking myself out to dinner. I told her that you didn't like a wide variety of foods, the ballet or concerts.

"But Michael's not the issue here, *you* are. What stops *you* going out and seeing and doing things?"

"I don't know."

"Yes you do."

"Well, I would be scared to go out all alone. I've always gone out with Michael. I was always part of a couple."

"Does the other part of the couple always have to be your husband? Could it be someone else?"

"Are you suggesting I get a lover?" I asked lightly.

"No, I am suggesting you ask a friend, for starters."

"I can't think of anyone that I would like to go out with. Just about everyone I know is tied up in some way with Michael. They are the wives of his friends. I couldn't relax and just be me."

"Then," said Anne, "ask for a new friend. Put it out there."

"Ask who? Out where?" Anne was going all woo-woo on me.

"Out into the Universe. Then expect it, intend it and feel as though you already have it."

"Just feel good and it will show up – huh?"

"Something like that," said Anne, smiling.

"I don't think my problems will be solved by a couple of nights out on the town."

"No, but it's a way to start creating a different life. Start small. Start having fun, get happy and find out where it leads you. Your homework this week will be to make a list of what you want and why. Write a joy list."

"Like a bucket list?" I asked.

"Not a bucket list. That's more like a reminder that life is short and you are going to die. Make the list about joy, make it about expansion and growth, make it about fun and freedom. Just write down what you want and why."

"And how to get it?" I asked.

Anne shook her head firmly. "Definitely not. Just write what you want and why. Make it limitless, anything you want, no financial concerns, no judgments, no worrying about what I or anybody else might think about it. Just write down your wildest dreams, everything you want and why you want it."

"Why not how?" I asked.

"It will mess you up. I'll explain later, or you will discover it for yourself."

I went home and set to work on writing a list of everything I wanted and why. I was tempted to write about how I could get what I wanted, but every time I thought about *how* something might happen, the momentum of my inspiration and enthusiasm slowed. Instead, I felt only doubt and discouragement, so I stopped thinking about how altogether. The only thing that mattered was what I wanted and why.

Chapter 16

A Powerful Idea

I drew a line down the middle of the page and put 'what' at the top on the left and 'why' on the right. I wrote down every simple and extravagant idea I could think of. After a while, I realized the why column had the same words in it: it would be fun, I would feel better or it would be exciting. So, was everything I wanted to be, do or have because I would feel better? That was interesting.

I thought about the picture in Anne's office, the one painted by Grandma Moses. I went online and googled images of her paintings. I picked the one I liked most and saved it as wallpaper on my computer so that every time I turned it on, I would be reminded that a woman can do anything at any age if she is enthusiastic about it. It occurred to me, that as a forty-eight year old woman, I was really just a spring chicken. It also occurred to me that I would probably always want to work.

I used to envy those women who could meet regularly with their friends to chat, have their hair done or go shopping. I saw them in the morning at the coffee shops in their sports gear, settling in while I hurried past to buy my coffee to take to work. I don't envy them now. I need a purpose and I need to feel useful.

I was beginning to get the hang of this 'what if' and 'wouldn't it be nice' and 'focus on good things' way of looking at life. Winter had passed and there had been a few nights when we didn't need to put the heating on. Sparrows started to gather at dawn and dusk in a small tree by the patio.

Their excited twittering was a sign to me that things were about to get better. I made sure I sat out there in the evenings to hear them and to admire the new dandelions in the lawn. I began thinking about living in a warmer climate. It was the first time I had ever considered living somewhere else.

Early one morning, I was standing at the kitchen sink, eating toast and jam and reading over my list of what I want and why I want it. I had told Anne about all the things I can't do: art, sport, music or anything creative with my hands. What can I do? I looked at my joy list and something jumped out at me. I saw 'write a book'. Why? It would bring in an income if it was published and I could work less. It would be useful, it would help others, it would be empowering to describe myself as a best-selling author, it might make me rich and because, simply and most importantly, it would be fun.

The evening before, I had been online trying to find a book on the management of childcare centers. I was frustrated because I hadn't found what I wanted. I remembered that Anne had said months ago that there was 'a book in that'. She had been suggesting that I write a book but I hadn't heard her because I was focused on my own misery. At the time, I hadn't been bored enough to make room for any new ideas.

Now that there was room, I could write a book about something I knew a lot about! My heart began to thump. Writing was something I was good at in school. I knew my subject and I was passionate about good childcare. Maybe I hadn't found the right book because there wasn't one. Well, I could write it, and I could fill a gap in the market. I sat at the kitchen bench with a note pad and wrote down a list of questions. What makes a great childcare center, what makes staff loyal and active, what keeps children happy, what makes parents grateful? What mistakes do administrators make, what mistakes do childcarers make? What do they do well? How could everything work better? How could professional development be integrated into the center? How could administrators manage the budget more easily and ensure that parents pay on time? Each question created an idea for a new chapter.

Over the following weeks, I wrote notes and organized the structure of the book. I read online articles on the subject. I set out to write a book that someone in my profession would need and appreciate. I talked into the recorder on my phone every time I got an idea and followed through with that idea as soon as I could, when I was alone. Now I could really feel the benefit of your absence.

Over dinner one night, I told you I was planning to write something about childcare. You smiled distractedly and I could tell you thought it was going to be some kind of pamphlet. You didn't offer to read it or make suggestions but you did show some interest when I said I was going to need some time during the weekends to write or travel and I hoped you wouldn't mind. You told me you were perfectly fine with that. Of course you were; it meant more time with your girlfriend.

On the surface, my life looked almost the same. I went to work every Monday, Tuesday, Thursday and Friday. On Wednesday mornings, I still took care of your parents. I saw the kids often and met my playgroup friends for coffee. I told them nothing about myself, although I was occasionally tempted to be the center of their attention. Then, when I watched them gossip with each other, I realized it was something I no longer wanted to do. If they talked that way about other people, they would talk that way about me. And I no longer cared if they did.

I started to do something else on Wednesday afternoons and on weekends. I went out on my own. I started to travel, and travelling alone was easier than I thought. Sometimes I stayed away overnight and it was your turn to be at home alone. I visited childcare centers of different sizes, in inner and outer suburbs and in rural and remote areas all over the state. I went everywhere I could think of and saw parts of the country I had never seen before. I saw problems in childcare centers that needed fixing.

I saw that sole parents, parents on welfare, working parents, parents of children with special needs, migrants, refugees and non-English speaking parents all needed extra support. The more I travelled, the more I observed and learned. I was a long way from my cozy, cloistered center in the middle class suburbs and I was both troubled and fascinated. I wanted to do something about the problems I saw.

I hired a virtual secretary named Anita who typed up my thoughts from my recorder in the evenings and emailed the transcripts to me every morning. It worked very well. Together, we wrote to organizations, colleges and universities here and overseas to gather more information on effective childcare management. I completed the first three chapters of the book and sent them to a professor at the Institute of Early Childhood. We spoke on the phone and she promised to look over my material and offer suggestions.

I was on my way.

Chapter 17

Now I Get It

One weekend, late in August, I went to a writers' workshop in Sydney. I spent the first evening in my hotel room and watched three movies, drank champagne and ate chocolate. It was fun. I felt like the housewife in the movie 'Goddess'.

During the workshop the following day, I was inundated with information from experts in the publishing industry. I learned that social media has re-written the rules of the publishing business. I learned about self-publishing, e-publishing and publishing on demand. I learned about a machine called the 'Espresso Book Machine' that can produce a book in six minutes. I learned about book proposals and the role of literary agents and editors. It was a really interesting day.

That evening, I sat by myself in the crowded hotel restaurant. Everyone seemed to be in couples or in groups and I was the only one alone. I felt self-conscious so I looked at messages in my phone while I waited for my meal. The waiter asked me if someone could share my table and I said, "Yes, certainly." A young man sat down opposite me and thanked me. I recognized him from the conference. He had asked the speakers several interesting questions about publishing.

Initially I was uncomfortable, not knowing whether to ignore him or talk to him. He smiled and said, "I saw you at the conference. How about we introduce ourselves and talk to each other?"

His direct approach made me smile. He was about ten years younger than me and had nice eyes. Soon we were happily having our meal and sharing our writing projects. It was easy. I told him about my book. He thought it sounded worthwhile and hoped it would be a success. He wanted to hear my ideas about his book. He made me feel like an interesting person. He told me what he knew about marketing and suggested that I start a blog. I had no idea how to go about that so he recommended someone in Melbourne who could help. It was a new, fascinating world.

I have always been a little brown bird, not particularly attractive and certainly not the kind of woman any man, especially a married man (other than Sam), would choose to have an affair with, so I was relaxed. I think my glass of wine helped. We talked about books and publishing. Neither of us mentioned our private lives. I didn't want to return to my hotel room, so I had a second glass of wine, something I never do. We finished our meals and lingered over coffee. We paid our bills, got up and left the restaurant. We headed for the lift together and laughed, because it was awkward.

When we were alone in the lift, we stood silently looking at the numbers above the door the way most people do. Then he leaned over and kissed me gently. I hesitated at first, surprised, and then I leaned into it. It was a perfect kiss. He put his arms around me and I could feel him hard against me. We went to my room, and Mike, I have to say, sex with him was different from anything I had experienced with you. Two men with basically the same equipment and yet this sexual encounter was so extraordinarily different. Not only that, there was so much more of it! All I will say is he was a very energetic young man and by round four I was thinking, 'let me go to sleep, I'm tired'. You and I hadn't made love more than once a night since your early thirties. It was fun to experience that again.

He dressed some time during the night, kissed me and said "Thank you for your beauty." I smiled sleepily and said, "Likewise." There was no exchange of numbers. His last words to me were, "I look forward to seeing you on the cover of your best-selling book." I smiled up at him and said, "Likewise." I never saw him again. Do I regret it? Not one bit. It was fabulous. That man became my secret inspiration. I wanted to get my picture on the cover of my book as soon as possible.

And you know what, darling? Revenge had nothing to do with it. It was not about two wrongs making a right. It had nothing to do with you. I didn't think about you at all. Not once. Not until the following morning when, lying in bed, I remembered who I was and what I wanted. I am not telling you this to hurt you, Mike; I just want you to know what I learned from it. I didn't have to tell you at all. It could have been my secret, but I am telling you for two reasons: firstly, I get why you would want to have sex with someone else and secondly, I believe it will be easier for you to let me go if you know I have been unfaithful.

I lay in bed that morning, thinking about what happened and how and why it happened. I thought, now I get it; I understand how you could risk everything, your home, family and reputation for something as different and delightful as that. I can understand it, because it had been fun and exciting for me. It was great sex. I imagined that your girlfriend made you feel younger and stronger, in the same way that the young man made me feel beautiful and desirable.

I got it. It was all about the way she made you feel, the way I no longer make you feel. I understood how you might want to have sex with someone else. I even understood how exciting it must have felt to be in a new relationship. What I couldn't get, or get over, was that you lied to me daily for months. How could that have been fun? How could that still have been worth it? I have trouble understanding and accepting that, even now.

After the workshop, I spent another day in Sydney, visiting childcare centers and talking to people. That evening, I took a taxi out to the airport. The plane I boarded was taxiing out to the runway for the flight home when I noticed that the young woman to my left, in the middle seat, was breathing hard and holding her husband's hands so tightly that he was trying to pull her fingers away. I could see that she was at serious risk of becoming hysterical so I looked forward and leaned slightly in her direction.

"You know, flying is like great sex," I said softly.

She turned to look at me, astonished.

"What did you say?" she asked.

"It goes better if you lie back and relax," I replied and gave her a mischievous grin. "Just breathe and tell yourself the pilot wants to get there too."

She stared at me and then smiled slowly. I was relieved because I had spoken without thinking. She could have been horrified; she could have thought I was a pervert. I could have made things worse, but fortunately, she smiled and then asked me where I was headed.

"I have just been to a writers' workshop and learned lots about book publishing. Now I am on my way home." I began to tell her about my experience at the workshop.

A minute later, she looked out the plane window and saw that we were up in the air.

"You distracted me, didn't you!" she exclaimed.

"Yes," I said, smiling. "I was afraid that if you had hysterics, I wouldn't get home today." She laughed and introduced her husband. She smiled at him and held his hands, gently this time. I sat back, closed my eyes and thought about great sex, of very recent, really, really great sex.

My Sydney experience made me think about dating. I considered the possibility of seeing someone. You were; why couldn't I? It would be a boost to my ego. On the other hand, I would have to lie to you. I would have to deceive you while I was living with you and I would have to deceive the other man. I would have to involve someone else in my already complicated life. I would have less time for myself and my writing. The whole idea quickly went sour. It wasn't what I wanted and frankly, I couldn't be bothered.

When I got home, I employed a young man named Ryan to teach me the ropes about websites, blogs, social media, Facebook and all the other things that help people become known to other people. I set up a blog about childcare management, which doesn't sound all that important until you discover how many million children are in care at any one time. I started writing down my ideas in the blog and I felt just like Julie, in the movie 'Julie and Julia'. I started getting some readers. It was encouraging to discover that there were people out there who wanted to hear what I had to say. My horizons began to expand and I started exchanging ideas with childcare managers all over the world.

I started singing "The mornin' sun is shinin' like a red rubber ball."

Chapter 18

Down A Snake And Up A Ladder

It was a beautiful day in September. I drove to my favorite bookshop, parked my car opposite and crossed the road. As I stepped up onto the curb, I tripped and fell flat on my face. I have no memory of the fall itself. One second I was stepping up, the next I was face down on the footpath. I lay there, too surprised to move. My face stung, my knees hurt and I groaned in pain.

People gathered around and helped me up. They asked me if I was all right and if there was anyone with me who could help. I felt blood running down my face. I had cut my forehead and bitten through my bottom lip. My nose was sore and my knees were grazed and bleeding. A woman said, "Let me take you in there." She pointed to a coffee shop nearby. I agreed to go with her to get away from the concerned stares. I saw myself in the shop window and I looked a mess. Blood was running from my right eyebrow into my eye, and from my lip down my chin and onto my shirt.

The woman took me to a quiet table in the corner of the café, sat me down and asked the waiter for two cappuccinos and some water. She used the water and a napkin to wipe my face. I wanted to get away because I was embarrassed, but I was also comforted by her kindness. She told me her name was Sue.

"See what happens when you keep your eyes on the handsome men around here? You don't watch where you're going and you fall over!" she said.

I smiled, in spite of my pain.

"But that one was especially handsome!" I replied and she laughed.

Sue made it easy for me to get my dignity back. She invented a funny story to explain my fall.

"Well, you see there was this very handsome Spaniard…" she said.

I added to the story and soon it got a bit crazy and we had to stop. My face was still bleeding and I had to hold my split lip to stop it bleeding when I laughed. Sue and I agreed that Melbourne has great bookshops. We mourned the demise of Borders. We also agreed that Spanish men are more handsome than other men and Spaniards on horseback are the most handsome of all.

Sue sipped her cappuccino and encouraged me to have mine. I did, gingerly, from one side of my mouth. It tasted good. It reminded me of all the comforting food my mother gave me when I was small and sick in bed. It almost made the world right again. Then Sue looked at her watch and apologized, saying that she needed to be somewhere. She took out a piece of paper and wrote her name and number on it, and I thanked her for her kindness.

"Let me know how you are; I would like to hear," she said as she turned to leave.

I stayed in the café for a while and had another coffee. It's hard to describe to you how I felt, Mike. I was in pain, yet pleased. I watched people come and go and for the first time in a long while, I took some time to sit and do nothing, absolutely nothing. It was lovely. People looked at my face and looked away again. To them I was just a woman who had fallen over recently. It was nothing important, nothing to take them away from their own concerns. Falling over reminded me of playing snakes and ladders as a child. Sometimes you slide down a snake and feel discouraged because you're getting nowhere in the game. Then the next minute you climb a ladder to an exciting new place on the board. I had fallen over and made a friend.

That evening, you looked at my face and offered to cook dinner. You sat me down carefully and looked after me. You kissed me on an unbruised part of my forehead, do you remember? I felt blessed. I decided to add that to my list of positive aspects about you. I was climbing a ladder up the board again. Then you went to another room to take a phone call and I remembered why I was thinking of leaving you. Disappointed, I slid quietly down the snake.

A few days later, I called Sue and let her know that I was doing well. It was nice to hear her friendly voice. On impulse, I asked if I could return the favor and buy her a cup of coffee. She suggested we meet at a nearby café and when I arrived, she greeted me as though we had known each other for years. Sue is a happily married woman, a grandmother several times over and a semi-retired chartered accountant. You would have liked her, Mike. She was someone with whom I could just relax. For me, that was rare. I had that connection with Mum, with Judy and with you and your Dad, a connection where I felt completely understood, accepted and appreciated. In my world, I work with colleagues, staff, parents, wives of your friends and some friends of my own, but I was on tip-toe, watching what I said, being politically correct and feeling a little on the outer. I have always worried about what other people thought, which meant I never did anything brave. However, with Sue, I could be me.

One afternoon, not long afterward, you called to say you were going to be home very late. I prowled the house for a while before I realized I was being ridiculous. Surely there was something I could do. I wasn't in the mood to write or do research. I wanted to do something different and I didn't want to do it by myself, so I rang Sue.

"Are you free for a night out tonight?" I asked her.

"Sure," she said, "What do you have in mind?"

"How about dinner and a movie?"

"You're on!"

So we went out for dinner, saw a very forgettable romantic comedy, had a coffee and went home. It was the first time I had ever done something so spontaneous and fun.

"This sure beats going to the movies with my husband," said Sue. "He likes gory thrillers and war movies and he groans or sleeps through anything he considers soppy."

I laughed because I knew exactly what she meant. We talked about our husbands' reluctance to take us to the ballet, live theatre, galleries or exhibitions.

"This was fun," I said, "let's do it more often."

Sue agreed. "How about I find something for us to do next time? What do you like?"

"I want to learn to enjoy a lot of things, so you can choose whatever takes your fancy and we can make it up as we go along."

"Done!" she said.

Sue bought tickets to the ballet for our second night out. It was a night when you happened to come home early. I was dressed and ready when you walked in the front door. It pleased me to be able to say that your dinner was on the stove and that I was going out. I had seldom gone out in the evenings without you. I saw the dismayed look on your face and chose to believe that you had hoped to spend the evening with me, but really, I was too excited about the prospect of going out to care what you were feeling.

The ballet was glorious. It was lovely being out at night in the city amongst the crowds, watching how people dress up to sit in the dark and watch someone else dancing. The live performance was better than I could possibly have imagined. Sue and I talked afterwards about all our impressions. I also told her about my book. She listened carefully and made some interesting suggestions about accounting and management. She was encouraging and supportive. "I'll be your cheer squad, your support team," she said.

From then on, we met for coffee every second Wednesday afternoon. I laid out my ideas for the book and she gave me suggestions. She read the chapters as I went along, underlined sentences that didn't work well and ideas that needed elaboration. She always allowed me to feel that it was my book and that my decisions were final.

Sue told me that her husband was in Rotary and on various committees, which gave her some evenings free. She was devoted to him and spoke fondly of him. We were both happy that we knew no one in common. We could talk about almost anything. However, Anne Holmes had suggested that I not talk about you until I was able to do it with a positive spirit, so I didn't talk about you at all. I wasn't there yet.

After Sue and I had been out, I slept better. It was as though having a new friend partially compensated for your absences. I went to sleep looking forward to going out again. Having fun with a friend might seem like a small step to you, but it was a big leap for me.

Over the next few months, Sue and I competed to please and astonish each other with our choices of evenings out. I took her to a Pink concert and we jumped and screamed with everyone around us. On the way home, we sang 'So What!' as loudly as we could and people in nearby cars stared at us. Next, Sue took me to a Spanish horse show to watch handsome Spaniards. I took her to the National Gallery and she took me to a burlesque show. I took her to the 'Vagina Monologues' and she took me to 'Puppetry of the Penis'. I had discovered the art of having outrageous fun.

And it all had nothing to do with you.

I began to think about how I wanted my life to be if we separated. Was I going to do what I had always done; did I want to do something completely different or a little of both? I started adding things to my joy list: travel to distant shores, more books, new friends and a different career.

A beautiful future was beginning to take shape.

Chapter 19

Ask And It Is Given

At our next session, I told Anne I was astonished that no sooner had I needed a friend when one appeared. What was that?

"Interesting isn't it!" said Anne. "You asked, the Universe set it up and you became ready to receive what you asked for."

"Whoa!" I exclaimed. "That's a bit woo-woo and out-there for me."

"But maybe worth thinking about," said Anne. "In the meantime, tell me how you have been doing with the word 'should'.

I told her that for the first week, my left wrist was red and sore, but after a while, I automatically shifted my words to want, could and would like, which meant that I was beginning to say new and more positive things. I had begun to discover optimism and enthusiasm. I was enthusiastic about my writing, my new social life and about the possibilities in my future.

I mentioned the young man at the writers' workshop. Anne asked me why I was telling her and I replied that I wanted to know what she thought about it.

"Well, what do *you* think about it?" she asked.

I said that it had been fun and that I had learned a lot.

"Well, then, we can leave it there. If it ain't broke, don't fix it, so let's not spend our time on that. Let's talk about what you would like to do next."

"Well, I don't have any intentions of repeating that, not immediately anyway," I said smiling.

"Okay, so let's focus on what you do intend. Remember, someone who is focused on what they want is more powerful than millions who aren't."

I asked her what she meant and she suggested I read books about Mother Teresa, Eleanor Roosevelt or Helen Keller. They were all women who accomplished great things over the age of forty.

"How has it been going at home?" Anne asked.

I said that I was more relaxed and you were home just a little more often than you had been for the past five months. In fact, things between us were quite good and I was strangely happy and also eager for more, but…

Anne interrupted quickly; she pointed in the upstream direction and made me start again.

"You don't always have to tell me how it is," she said. "You don't have to focus on the truth. You could tell me how you would like it to be."

"But then that's not true and I would be making it up. That's just lying."

"Like the handsome Spaniard?" She grinned at me.

I laughed and agreed with her. That story was certainly better than the truth. It was a bit like 'The Life of Pi'. The fiction was more bearable than the reality.

"Then tell me only what you want and why. In the past you have been very good at going back and explaining, defending and justifying where you are and why it is the way you *don't* want it to be. I would like you to stop doing that and tell me instead how you want it to be with no ifs, buts or maybes."

I told her that I was going out more and was pleased to be going out regardless of what you were doing. I had more control of my life. I had almost decided to leave you and be happy. I hadn't worked out how to leave you and still keep my home, so I wasn't ready quite yet. She agreed and suggested I wait until I was one hundred percent ready. I was making progress with the book. I asked her why it was sometimes easy to write and sometimes it just felt like a drag.

"Firstly," she said, "I suggest you be careful who you tell about your book."

"Why?" I asked. I was worried that she would disapprove of me having told Sue.

"Telling others about a new project can make you vulnerable to people's negative opinions. While it is a small seed, protect it, nurture it and watch it grow, but don't give it to anybody else to crush.

"Some people will be jealous; some won't believe you can do it or won't want you to do it. Some might say it's already been done and that a book on that subject wouldn't be interesting. This could tap into any feelings of doubt you may have and entrench them further. There are people who will say things like 'but what makes you think you can write a book? You haven't written one before' or 'why would you want to do that?' with a tone in their voice that implies that your book would be a waste of time. They will say things like 'it's too hard, too expensive, too complicated to get published' and they will tell you that thousands of people write books every year that never get published and imply that yours won't either. If you don't tell people, you won't have to listen to any of that. If you do tell anyone, make it one trusted and supportive friend and even then, I suggest waiting until the book is well on the way to being written, when nothing anyone says can dissuade you or make you write what *they* think you should write.

"My second suggestion is to only write when you are in a great mood and you feel inspired. Don't write when it feels like an effort. Do something else. Go for a walk, clean the house, chat with a friend, but don't write. Get happy and then write. The speed with which you finish the book is unimportant. An inspired book is always a better book and it will also sell better because people reading it will feel inspired."

I told Anne that Sue knew about the book and she had been very supportive, but that I hadn't told you. I wanted to keep my book a secret from you for many reasons. Then I told her about what I had been learning from other childcare centers, particularly those in the poorer areas of the city, and in remote areas.

Anne looked at me and smiled. "Stop looking at the problems," she said.

I was surprised. Was she suggesting that I turn a blind eye to everything that was wrong with childcare?

"But if I don't look at the problems, how can I solve them?"

"I didn't say don't look at the problems..." Anne said. I started to object. That was exactly what she said.

"What I meant was, look at them briefly and then turn your attention toward solutions as soon as possible, because you can't fix a problem by focusing on the problem. Turn your attention toward the solution. For the next month, that can be your homework. Start with problems in your own life. Recognize the problem and turn your attention immediately to the solution, any solution you can think of."

So I did. The problem was that you were not home. The solution was that I could write or go out and have some fun. The problem was that I didn't have enough time to work on my book. The solution was that I could work one day less per week at the center. I talked to my assistant about job-sharing and she was very interested. The problem was that our finances would change if I took time off. I could find ways to save money. I cancelled the cable TV and the newspaper deliveries. I made more meatloaf and fewer roasts. I took more notice of specials in the supermarket and lower petrol prices. I became more vigilant about turning lights off and I wore a jumper instead of putting on the heater. It was actually fun finding ways to save money because each little bit I saved represented one step closer to happiness.

It felt good to identify a problem and to turn my focus immediately to a solution. It was surprising to see how a solution, even if it didn't end up being the one I finally went with, headed me in the right direction. One idea piggy-backed another until the best solution appeared. Sometimes the problem and solution occurred at the same time and a sort of mini-miracle happened. Life began to move more smoothly for me and it got better and better. No sooner had I asked for something than it appeared. Maybe Anne was on to something with her woo-woo stuff.

You came home earlier in the evenings. We took walks along the bike track into town and across parks. We talked a little, but our walks were generally quiet. We both had subjects that we could not discuss so there were two very big, grey elephants trailing along behind us. As we walked, I looked at your quiet, troubled face and wished I could say, "You can tell me now. I am over the worst of it. You can tell me now. It will be okay." And still, I said nothing. You mentioned you would be attending the real estate annual conference in Perth in early December and I made a mental note of that.

While I think of it, do you remember sweetheart, after I made you watch the movie 'The Lake House', you couldn't work out how his time-frame could catch up to hers, but you had to admit that it was a good film 'for a chick flick'? Then later, we saw Sheldon on 'The Big Bang Theory' reduce the movie to 'love with a time-travelling letter-box', which made us laugh. Both of us, without knowing the other was doing the same thing, went out and bought the whole season of 'The Big Bang Theory' just so we could watch Sheldon say it again. We kept both DVD sets. I don't know why. Perhaps it was to remind ourselves that on some things we thought alike. Now I am now taking mine with me.

I also remember how you got tearful at Sheldon's reaction to Penny's Christmas present of the napkin with Leonard Nimoy's DNA on it. It was our favorite scene. I can remember things like that now and they make me smile, whereas I used to think I would lose all those lovely memories when I lost you.

I now understand how Humphrey Bogart could say to Ingrid Bergman in 'Casablanca', so calmly and so knowingly, "We will always have Paris."

Chapter 20

The Tipping Point

Over the past five months, Eleanor started coming over more often. She came on simple pretexts, to bring me a bunch of flowers or something she had baked, to have a cup of coffee or just to chat. I could tell that she worried about me and I wished she wouldn't. She mentioned to me one day, about three months ago, that she hadn't seen you and me together recently. I took a deep breath and decided that this was probably a good time to tell her what was happening. We sat down together.

"I have something to tell you," I said.

"No, you don't," she whispered, "I already know."

She started to cry. She cried for a long time and I held her close.

"I saw them in a restaurant about two months ago, Mum. I didn't know what to do and I hoped that it was a one-off. I couldn't tell you, I am so sorry."

"It's okay, possum. It's okay. I already knew."

Eleanor was going into a Chinese restaurant to make a take-away order when she saw you. You were sitting at a table in a corner, holding hands with a woman. Eleanor left immediately and sat in her car outside the restaurant until you came out, and she watched the two of you walk arm-in-arm up the street to your car. She didn't follow you further. She was crying and shaking and afraid to drive in that state. She had lost the father she believed in and had found a father who was a lying bastard. Those were her words, not mine, Mike. It had been hard for her to be with me because she had a secret she wanted to share, but couldn't. She was afraid of making things worse. She, like me, was hoping it would go away. I listened to her while she expressed the confusion, the fear and anger I had experienced in the previous eight months. We talked for a long time and since that day I have sometimes wished I could have recorded her words, just so you could hear what our daughter went through because of you.

"How could he do this to you, Mum?" she asked.

I told her I didn't know why and that I was thinking of leaving you because, despite everything I had tried, you hadn't stopped seeing that woman. Then I told her that her grandmother had left the house to her and her brother. She was shocked and worried. I asked her what she wanted to do, and she asked me what *I* wanted her and Henry to do.

"Mum, it's not my house, even if it is legally," she said. "It's yours and you should decide what happens to it, though I admit I would like to get rid of my student loans and get into the housing market before I get much older."

I realized then that while I might be sentimental about my home, Eleanor was thinking of her own future and her old home wasn't that important to her. I was both disappointed and relieved. The time had come when I had to think about how I felt about my home. I still loved it but it was now becoming a stumbling block. I might have to consider my future without it. Eleanor and I agreed to talk to Henry about the possibility of them selling the house and paying off their student loans. They could use some of the money to buy something small for me to live in, which they could sell when I croak. We have always liked the term 'croak'. It made us able to talk about death in a nonchalant way.

"What about Dad? Where will he live? Do you think he will buy the house? If we don't help him, he will be left with nothing," said Eleanor.

"I don't know," I replied. "That is something he will have to work out for himself. He has investments."

That evening at dinner, Eleanor and I told Henry that you had been seeing another woman for a while and that I was thinking of leaving you. Henry listened calmly and continued eating his dinner. I asked him what he thought.

Henry looked up. "Marriage is an outdated institution," he said. "There should just be a contract that says you share the raising of the children and then when that's done, it should be up for re-negotiation. You guys should re-negotiate, I reckon. It's about time you two did something interesting." He went back to eating. Just like Henry, unemotional and blunt.

Eleanor and I looked at each other and smiled. Maybe I was, for the first time, doing something interesting. We spoke to him about the house.

"Whatever," said Henry. "I don't want the responsibility now. I'll get my share of it when you croak anyway. What's for dessert?"

"As long as you'll be okay," said Eleanor, anxiously looking at me.

Henry gave a nonchalant shrug in agreement. He has always tried so hard to be cool, but I could see that he was concerned.

A memory of him came to mind. He was a small boy standing in the back yard wearing gumboots and holding a little plastic hammer. He was waiting for you to help him make a cubby house, but you were busy and had forgotten. He looked anguished and disappointed. I watched him through the kitchen window and knew that he didn't want me to help him. He wanted his dad. I went to get you and insisted you stop what you were doing and go look after him. You did and the two of you spent the rest of the day hammering and sawing. Henry was beyond happy. He came in later, dirty and tired, and threw his arms around me in a great big hug. Then he spread his arms wide and grinned, exclaiming, "I love you THIS big!"

That memory stood out from all those other memories of him down at the police station, or vomiting helplessly into the toilet or throwing abuse at us in his teens. Once again, he was my darling little boy who loved being helpful. So I asked his advice about my computer and he went off to look at it.

"Why didn't you tell us before about Dad?" asked Eleanor later, as we washed the dishes together.

"I wanted to be able to manage it in my own way," I replied. "At first I hoped it would stop, and then after a while when it didn't, I began to hope that the marriage would stop."

"Do I have to be nice to his girlfriend?" she asked.

"You don't have to hate her if you don't want to. You can figure it out as you go along."

"What are you going to do now, and when? Please don't leave it too long," said Eleanor. "I don't think I could cope with waiting to see what happens. I want to see that you are happy and well taken care of."

Eleanor's words tipped the balance.

Strike Three.

If you want to know what finally made me decide to leave you, I can tell you this. I was standing in the kitchen washing dishes with Eleanor and I realized I had to be strong for her and Henry. I had to make a decision. If my family was going to fall apart, it would be on my terms, not on yours and definitely not on your girlfriend's.

Ultimately, my decision to leave you had nothing to do with you or with what you had done. It didn't even have anything to do with me or what I wanted. It had everything to do with our kids. I didn't want them to suffer while they waited to see what we would do. I wanted my son and daughter to be happy. It was as simple as that. They would both be happier once a decision was made one way or the other. I needed to come to a decision quickly, for their sakes.

Eleanor and I talked at length about the house and made a plan. I hugged her and reassured her that she was loved beyond measure and that I wasn't planning to disappear into the wide blue yonder like someone in a movie.

"The people I love are here," I said. "Why would I go somewhere else? I might take a holiday, but I am not going anywhere permanently."

"Maybe you should get another dog or a cat," suggested Eleanor.

I shook my head though I understood her reasoning. All her life, until nearly a year ago, we had dogs, mostly Labradors. Eleanor especially had loved them all, but would I have a dog now? No way.

"Thank you darling, but no," I said. "I am just about to get some freedom and I don't want to be tied down to a pet. It wouldn't fit in with my future as I am planning it."

I told her about my book, my savings, my plans for long service leave and my joy list.

"The last thing you need now, my possum," I said, "is a bored, elderly mother living on her own with nothing but a dog for company, ringing you twice a day to find out how you are and why you don't come to see her more often."

Eleanor smiled and agreed that having an independent, happy mother was exactly what she needed. We decided that I had to get organized before I jumped ship. Then, her face crumpled.

"I will miss Christmas," she said sadly.

"We will still have Christmas," I said. "It's just that this year we will have to do it on a different day. I know it won't be the same, but maybe someday down the track we can create a new Christmas tradition."

"But it won't be the same," whispered Eleanor as she rested her head on my shoulder. I hugged her and said, "No, you're right. It won't be the same." We stood there together for a long while.

Christmas was always a big affair. I made sure of it. Amanda and her family always came down from Sydney and we had your parents, assorted family members, my mother and any of the kids' friends who had nowhere to be. It would be so lonely not to have anywhere to go on Christmas day. Many of Eleanor's and Henry's friends were caught between parents and step-parents, being fought over, or more sadly, not being fought over, at Christmas. So we always had a big, rowdy crowd and it was fun.

I will and I won't miss Christmas. The kids and I will just have to make it up as we go along. Maybe down the track there will be grandchildren and we will create a new tradition. I hope so. This Christmas, I will remind myself that it is just another day and wherever I am, I will get through it. Eleanor said she and Henry would organize something with their friends who had nowhere to go. She knew they wouldn't want to spend it with you and your girlfriend.

I also told her that she and Henry could take what they wanted from the house when it is sold.

"What about Dad?" Eleanor asked again. I said I was pretty sure that your girlfriend probably wouldn't want anything of mine but I would make certain that everything special to you would be given to you.

I would keep working and life would go on. We would still meet for dinner. We would still have Christmas and I would still be their Mum.

Then, two months ago, I went to the Institute of Early Childhood to talk to the professor about my book. She had read the first three chapters and wanted to meet me. She was impressed with what I had written so far and asked if I had a publisher in mind. She asked whether I would mind her proposing my book to a local publisher. Would I mind?! Of course I wouldn't. I tried very hard to hide how thrilled I was. She promised to forward my chapters and to give the publisher my contact details.

She also asked if I would be interested in teaching classes for the Institute. My first reaction was fear. I had been a kindergarten teacher and I was now a childcare manager. I only spoke to three and four-year-old children and individually to their parents. How could I talk to adult students? I hadn't done any public speaking. The professor said that with my enthusiasm, I would find public speaking easy.

"I think you would be a natural," she said.

She told me about the Institute's curriculum and where she thought I might fit into it. The more she talked, the more I liked the idea of teaching others the importance of understanding the developmental needs of small children. I told her that I would be able to take up a part-time position next year. The classes started early in March so she suggested I do a public speaking course to get some practice in the meantime.

Darling, who would ever have thought that I could be both an author and a public speaker! The world has become a new and amazing place for me!

I needed to complete the book more quickly. I was working less, writing more, saving money and living a secret life. I joined Toast Masters and met new people. My first efforts at public speaking were pretty woeful, but with time, and by imagining the audience naked, I was able to relax and enjoy myself. I really had to stop worrying about what the audience might think about me and concentrate on the message I was giving them. I think you would have been amazed, Mike, to see your quiet, little brown bird standing in front of fifty people, talking about what matters to her. I like to think that you would have been impressed and proud.

Chapter 21

Life Is Supposed To Be Fun

"Tell me what has been going well this month," said Anne.

I told her about my book, about working less, about my nights out with Sue and how much fun we were having. I also told her about my conversation with the professor, joining Toast Masters, and my conversation about the house with the kids. It had been a busy and happy month.

When I had finished, Anne said, "Have you noticed that you didn't mention your husband once?"

I was astonished. Anne was right; I didn't mention you at all. I described my life, and how I was enjoying it, without even thinking about you. It was a very nice feeling. It was a tuned in, tapped in, turned on kind of feeling. It was as though you no longer factored into my equation of happiness.

"You sound inspired," said Anne. "It's the Universe showing you the next logical step and you getting to make it up as you go along."

"I do?"

"Sure, who else?"

"You mean I get to decide what I want?"

"Who else?"

Anne sat back and steepled her fingers in front of her. "What about living with the premise that life is supposed to be fun?"

"Huh? What is your definition of fun?" I asked. "I mean, what kind of world would it be if we all just spent our lives having fun?"

"Fun is doing what makes us happy," replied Anne. "It would be a wonderful world, don't you think, if we were all doing what made us happy?"

"But nothing would get done!" It sounded to me like she was describing an impossible world.

"The great thing about this world," continued Anne "is that people's ideas about what makes them happy are so diverse, and when people are truly happy, it doesn't occur to them to hurt anyone. Do you remember the man in Sydney who won the lottery and spent it on establishing a soup kitchen for the homeless? That was his idea of fun. It made him happy. There are people who are fascinated by waste water management and things that we don't want to have to think about, like post-mortem embalming.

"Think about Mother Teresa. Don't you think she had fun? She was working in the service of her Lord, which would have been very satisfying for her. That's another definition of fun. Very few people think that spending their life on a beach would be fun for more than a week." She paused. "Where did you get the idea that life was *not* supposed to be fun?"

I couldn't answer that. I didn't know many people who had fun on a regular basis. Most people had fun now and then on holidays or on the weekends, but no one I knew had lifestyles that I would consider fun, except one dear friend of mine who is a comedian on a cruise ship.

Anne read out various phrases in my journal and asked how those phrases made me feel. I quickly identified those that sent me upstream and those that allowed me to float downstream. She picked up from my notes that I was worried about what you thought, what Eleanor and Henry, my friends, your family, the people at work, the neighbors and even what your girlfriend thought.

"To make changes in your life, you need to make whatever anyone else thinks irrelevant *–totally irrelevant.* They are not you, and you are not them, so their opinions cannot matter at all. Worrying about what other people think nips ideas in the bud; it destroys inspiration and prevents progress. If you can practice the thought 'Whatever anyone else thinks is irrelevant' you will be on your way to where you want to be."

"But won't that turn me into a selfish person?" I asked. I couldn't believe that she was asking me to ignore the opinions of others.

"No. We don't stop being who we truly are, and who you truly are is a caring, kind and funny person. You care about others; you are a teacher to the core of your being and that will never cease to be. By thinking about what you want and going for it, you will serve as a role-model to others who will see that we all can be, do and have whatever we want."

"Why do we think that the opinions of others matter more than our own?" I asked. "How did we get so out of whack?"

"It started with our parents," replied Anne. "When we were very small, we learned that to be loved, we had to keep our parents happy and do what they wanted. If we did what we wanted instead, we were told we were selfish. Parents have given the word 'selfish' a bad name. Essentially, we are all selfish. We can only see the world through the eyes of our own selves.

"We can't make other people happy," continued Anne, "because most of the time they don't know what makes them happy, and if they do, it is generally temporary because what makes them happy one day doesn't make them happy the next. Do you remember when your children were small and they liked a particular cereal for breakfast? Did you buy it for them as a treat and then find that a month later they were sick of eating it and wanted something else?"

I nodded. I remembered how Eleanor and Henry loved Coco Pops and how, after a while, they asked for something different because they were so tired of them. I remembered feeling a little hurt because I thought I was giving them something special. There is no pleasing some people, I thought. I also remembered how much you liked coq au vin. I cooked it regularly until one day you said, "Again?" That was the last time I ever cooked it.

Anne continued: "You get to decide what makes you happy. Being happy will turn you into a more thoughtful, more joyous person. People will look at you in amazement and ask how you do it."

"Also," she added, "in future, write only downstream thoughts in your journal. Don't give the upstream thoughts any more air-time. Don't let them get momentum that will take you where you don't want to go. Write only what is delightful, interesting and helpful."

"Even if it's not true?" I asked.

"Even if it's not true," replied Anne firmly. "By the way, your journal makes interesting reading. There could be another book in that." She smiled and winked. "Just saying!" she said.

After that, writing in both my journal and my childcare book flowed more smoothly. No sooner had I had one happy thought than another followed, until I was experiencing a flood of happy thoughts and an avalanche of great ideas. I could even see the positive in things that once I would have thought of as terrible. For example, you showed *such* disinterest in me and what I was doing. Initially I was hurt, but I soon discovered that your disinterest gave me the space to explore possibilities in my life, to attend classes and go out with Sue. My secret life had become my own delicious little conspiracy. I hid from you my travels, appointments and progress with my book. That made it more exciting and it also made it easier to leave you.

Chapter 22

Making The Impossible Possible

Six weeks ago, Sue called to say that she was thinking of going to a Tony Robbins weekend seminar to walk on hot coals, and she asked if I wanted to come. We could share hotel expenses and it would be fun. I agreed immediately, although I was anxious about walking on hot coals. Then I thought, what better way to be jolted into believing that things could be different! I could make the impossible possible. Tony Robbins, the American motivational speaker, had about four thousand people in the convention center hanging on every word he said. He was a tall, impressive man standing on a dark stage with a spotlight and his own personal air-conditioner directed right at him. During the evening, he took us outside to the car park where huge piles of wood were burning and he explained what we would be doing later that night. I flip-flopped between terror and exhilaration as I listened to him.

At one o'clock in the morning, I was standing bare foot in front of a path of hot coals about a meter wide and six meters long. I watched Tony's staff shovel red-hot coals onto the grey ones and I wished they would stop. Fear spiked through me as I tried to focus on the soothing voice of Tony's crew member whose job it was to convince me to walk across. "Think cool moss," he said. I took the first step; then it was really easy to take the rest because the coals were very hot. At the other end, I wiped my feet on a patch of cool, wet lawn and another member of Tony's crew sprayed my feet with a hose. Sue had gone before me and was there waiting for me. We hugged with excitement. It was exhilarating; I felt invincible and I wanted to do it again, so I did.

It was after two in the morning by the time we got back to the hotel. Sue and I were elated and talked until dawn. We had learned so much and it was only the first day of the seminar. We had to be back in the conference center at nine in the morning but we didn't care. We couldn't sleep. We would sleep another day.

The next night, when we had settled into our hotel room, I decided to tell Sue about you.

"I have decided to leave my husband," I said.

"Tell me about it." Her tone was calm and encouraging.

I told her about what I saw nearly nine months ago, how you had been behaving, about working with Anne Holmes, about how miserable I had been and how I was now working my way up some kind of emotional ladder and floating down a stream. She sat and listened quietly without sympathy or lurid interest; just calm, quiet attention, which was just what I needed. She said she had always known there was something troubling me but wanted to wait until I was ready to mention it. I told her that Anne suggested not mentioning you to anyone until I could do it happily. I was ready to talk about you, but I was worried about what she might think. I was worried about what everyone might think.

"You don't need worry about what I think," she said. "If I know anything at all, it's that only the people in a relationship know what is going on in that relationship. If you need to leave him, you must have good reason. Here's an idea. How about I play devil's advocate? How about I say the kind of things you are worried that people might say?"

"You mean like a role play?" I asked.

"Yes, like that. I'll say all the things you don't want people thinking or saying and then you can react to them and see how it feels."

"Okay. Let's give it a go…" I paused and took a deep breath. "I'm leaving my husband."

"Oh dear no," said Sue. "You must stay with him! After all, boys will be boys and women are meant to stand by their man. It's not like you're the first woman that this has happened to. Why don't you just turn a blind eye? That's what wives do. After all, you might never meet anyone else if you leave. You'll be lonely forever. Nobody wants a woman over forty."

Sue's face was full of concern. I smiled. None of that worried me at all.

"Keep going." I said. "I am leaving my husband."

"What!" Sue exclaimed. "Just because he had one affair? Don't you think he deserves another chance? Everyone is entitled to one mistake."

This time, I exploded. I shouted at her. "One mistake! That's not fair. He has been seeing another woman for nearly a year as far as I know!" I got up and paced around the hotel room. Sue's words made me furious. "One mistake! That is *so* not fair! He made one mistake when he asked her for a drink, or took her out to dinner. He has lied to me every day for at least nine months! As far as I am concerned, he has made over 300 mistakes! And I don't think I have to give him another chance after 300 mistakes!"

I glared at Sue. I was shocked by the vehemence of my reaction. I was breathing hard; I went to get a drink of water and sat down again. Sue looked upset, which was the last thing I wanted.

"I think," she whispered, holding up her hand, "there is a danger in playing roles, of you thinking I am giving you *my* opinion. Please remember that I am making this up."

"I'm so sorry," I said. I went to sit with Sue and held her hand. I didn't mean to yell at her or frighten her. She smiled slowly at me and said, "Well, we know there's one answer you may need to practice before you mention it to others." She paused. "Are you really so worried about what other people think? Maybe they will surprise you."

"Maybe they will," I replied, "Perhaps I am not really ready to talk about leaving him yet. Not if I react like that… But I do want to know what will upset me; I do need to know where I might come unstuck. I know you don't mean it and I do appreciate you giving this role play thing a shot with me. Could we please do another one? I promise not to shout at you."

"Okay," said Sue slowly, "but remember that I am just saying what you are afraid people will say."

"Okay, let's try again.... I am leaving my husband." I sat and breathed deeply and looked expectantly at her.

"Let me try something else...." she said. " Yes, you should leave the bastard. All men are cheats and liars. Go for his throat. Go for his balls. Kick him to the curb. Leave him with nothing. You should have left him long ago. He has probably being screwing around for years. All men do! At least if he is screwing somebody else he is leaving you alone.... any better?"

I smiled. "One more, please. I think I am doing okay."

"Ok," said Sue. "Last try." She cleared her throat and managed to convey pious and pompous disapproval. "Marriage is a covenant made by God that no man or woman should put asunder. It is until death do you part. You would be committing a grievous sin by breaking the vow you made in front of Him (she raised her eyes to heaven) and the congregation. Your role is to remain with him through rich and poor, better or worse, to reproduce and endure and cook his dinner...we are but the chattels of men!"

"Enough!" I laughed.

"Obviously," said Sue, "those opinions don't upset you as much as you thought they would. So what are you really worried about?"

"Oh bother, now that I am no longer worried about what other people think, I can't find a single reason not to leave. Thank you *very* much!" We laughed together. The specter of public opinion faded. Everyone was free to think whatever they wanted. It was irrelevant to me. I was free to do whatever I wanted, whatever that was.

Sue laughed. “Let’s get back to your plans then.”

She asked me whether I had a passport so as soon as I returned home, I went to the post office to apply for one. At work, I made arrangements to take long service leave from December to March. At home, I picked a dandelion from the lawn. I then made an appointment with Ian, your solicitor friend, because there were things I needed to know.

But he and I have been friends since high school, I hear you say.

Yes, and now he is my solicitor – get over it.

Chapter 23

Zigging And Zagging

Anne and I continued to work on my thinking. She encouraged me to talk about what I wanted and to make lists of what I wanted and why. She encouraged me to focus on what was important to me and to those I cared about. I worked on my childcare book and as I write now, it is about half done. In my spare time, I have been working on a new, secret project. I am also reading the curriculum I will be teaching at the Institute. I am busy, I am happy and I am passionate about what I am doing.

I did all of this without you knowing anything about it. It is incredible to me that two people can live in the same house and not know what the other is doing. I was able to keep this from you because you were home so seldom and when you were there, you were distracted and unobservant. Your disinterest fueled my fierce determination. Every spare minute I had, I worked on my plans.

As the book developed and I received positive feedback from the readers of my blog, I walked around the house grinning to myself. It was just such a pity, my darling Mike, that of all the people I wanted to share my excitement with, you were the one person I couldn't tell. But I am beyond that now, that's how it is. I have stopped giving my attention to 'what was' or even 'what is'. I am entirely focused on 'what if', 'wouldn't it be nice if' and 'what next.'

What if the childcare book is published? What if it is a best-seller?

Wouldn't it be nice if it makes me rich and famous? What if it gives me choices? What if universities and colleges everywhere want it as a required text for their childcare courses?

What if my other new project takes off too?

Wouldn't it be nice if I could buy myself a lovely new home!

What if, what if, wouldn't it be nice if.

Just recently, I was home alone again. I was strangely restless. I needed to move and to get things done so I started to clean and tidy like I did months ago when I was angry, but this time the experience was very different. I wasn't just cleaning, tidying and rearranging; I was looking at every object and asking myself: Do I want it? Need it? Love it? I was sorting things to throw out. I wasn't putting everything back in its 'right place' anymore, I was making space. There were old wedding presents we never used, things we were given that I dutifully put away somewhere and there were so many things I didn't like but kept because I thought I had to. Now I no longer had to.

I wrapped old crock pots, clocks, ugly china, ornaments, linen and tea towels that your parents brought back from their caravan trips around the country. I cleaned out anything I didn't like and didn't want. By midnight, the house felt different. Several big bags of unwanted items were in the car ready to go to the Salvos. Every cupboard except yours had space. I had room to breathe, but I didn't want to be in my home anymore. I simply didn't want to be there. I was itching to get out all the time. I wanted to be somewhere else, doing something else. I was afraid that if I stayed in the same place, I would remain the same person I had always been, that the pull of my history would be too great. I started to look at my home as less of a haven and more of an anchor, holding me back and weighing me down. I was getting ready to be able to leave it. I was getting ready to leave you *and* my home.

But there was no way I was leaving it to you and your girlfriend.

I was changing inside and out. I couldn't listen to the radio anymore. Most of the music didn't match my mood so I made my own soundtracks with my favorite, powerful and uplifting songs. I made collections of the best songs I knew, from iTunes, and I played them at home and in the car. One of my old favorites was 'Gonna Get Along without Ya Now' (the Trini Lopes version). I sang it at the top of my voice every time I heard it. That song made me feel great. I also sang 'Survivor' by Destiny's Child.

My real life consisted of work, my book, my project, Sue, Eleanor, Henry and Anne. My life with you became a play, a performance. I felt removed from it, watching myself and watching you. When I was with you, I was an actress playing a role, just waiting for the play to end so that my real life could begin again.

We were *both* playing a role. You were, I believe, on the brink of deciding what to do next and you were struggling with that decision. I almost got the impression that the honeymoon period of your affair was over and that in some ways your girlfriend was becoming more of a problem to you than I was. I had no real evidence of it, I just liked believing it. You were home a little more often though, so maybe I was right. It was nice, but it was also a little inconvenient. I had become used to you not being there. I could write, I could go out with Sue, I could see our kids, I could make plans, I could make appointments, I could attend meetings and I could have fun. In fact, I became busier and less demanding – no, demanding is not the right word – less *wanting* of your time.

It was a time of strange changes when you zigged and I zagged. You were at home and I wasn't, I was at home and you weren't. If I believed in guardian angels, I would say they were working hard to help us avoid each other so our separation would be smooth and seamless.

When we were together it was okay, but it was impersonal because neither of us could talk about anything important. Our conversations were meaningless and we hid from each other in front of the television. I imagined your girlfriend pressuring you to tell me about your affair. I wished we could have had conversations where you told me that she didn't understand you. How ironic that would have been. I imagined you telling her that giving up your family, friends, home and reputation for her was not as easy as she might think. I could see sometimes in your face that you were struggling. Perhaps you didn't have anyone to talk to. I had Anne and Sue. As far as I knew, you had no one. You couldn't talk to your girlfriend because she was the cause and she couldn't be the cure, just as you were the cause of my pain, and couldn't be the cure. I had to find my own cure and I had found it, so we played our roles of husband and wife, parents, son and daughter-in-law, and it was all a performance.

It was when we went somewhere in the car that I could really feel the estrangement. Our car used to be a refuge where we could talk about anything. Cars were always an intimate place. In the early days, we hopped in the back seat at the drive-ins and parking spots, took country drives to get away from our parents and later, we drove to help our babies get to sleep. I feel sorry for the younger generation that doesn't know the thrill of going to the drive-in theatre.

Do you remember when you got your foot caught in the glove box? We laughed hysterically at the thought of a rescue crew working to get your foot out while trying to ignore the fact that you were naked from the waist down. Occasionally I think of those days, because those memories have the power to turn me on quickly and powerfully. Even when you're not here, I can recall those memories and they still work a treat.

But for the past ten months, the car was a silent prison and I could smell her perfume in it. I could feel when we got into the car that one of us wanted to say something, but neither of us could start, so we fell back into conversations like, 'Your mother is doing well', or 'Work has been very busy'. It was a strain, perhaps because you were planning to leave me or perhaps because I knew what I was about to do to you. So often, I wanted to lean across and put my hand on your thigh like I did many moons ago when we were dating, but I couldn't make that move now.

Your girlfriend puts her hand there now.

Chapter 24

The Waiting Universe

I kept working on the list of all the things I was planning to enjoy in my life. Anne suggested that I call it my joy list because the purpose of life is joy, and the only true measure of success is joy.

This is what I wrote:

I know this will sound insanely banal but the first thing that comes to my mind is garlic! Delicious, aromatic garlic! I can eat garlic. I can have garlic prawns, garlic bread, garlic salad dressing and garlic aioli. Actually sweetheart, I have put garlic in all my casseroles for years and you never noticed or complained, even though you claim to hate garlic. Just saying.

I can have mushrooms, fried, on pizza, in pasta or for breakfast. I can put caramelized onions in my mashed potato even though it turns the potato brown, which I know you hate. I can have eggplant, capsicum and zucchinis. I can eat asparagus without worrying about you not liking the smell. You know what I mean. I can eat biscuits in bed and blue cheese anywhere at any time. I can roast a piece of beef or lamb (with garlic!) so that it's still pink in the middle instead of cooking it to death the way you like it. I can put coriander and parsley on everything.

I love knowing that I don't have to cook at all if I don't want to. I no longer, ever, ever have to cook kidneys, liver or hard-boiled eggs. Have I ever told you how much I loathe the smell of liver? I no longer have to cook your mother's recipes. I can eat Spanish food, Thai food, Lebanese, Italian, African, Hungarian and Indian food – no more meat and three veg.

There's a whole culinary universe just waiting for me.

I can watch chick flicks without hearing your snorts of derision. I can cry at anything I want to, without you making faces at me. I can watch 'Poirot' and 'Miss Marple'! I can watch anything with Sandra Bullock in it. I can see the 'Bourne' series over and over again just because I love to watch Matt Damon. Your attitude always is 'but you know what's going to happen so how can it still be interesting?' Well, it just can!

I can watch 'Midsomer Murders' for John Nettles' beautiful blue eyes and the stunning English scenery, which I have now decided to see for myself (the scenery that is). I can watch 'Morse' for John Thaw. I can watch anything that has George Clooney or Denzel Washington in it! I never have to watch football on television ever again! I never have to pretend to care when your team loses. I don't have to know who won at Wimbledon or the PGA or the Australian Open or the Grand Prix. I don't have to pay any attention to any of that, ever again. I never have to watch the news if I don't want to – no more large doses of bad news every day. I can decide to leave the television off or I can decide not to have a television. What a concept!

I can go to foreign language movies with subtitles!

There's a whole cinematic universe just waiting for me.

I can enjoy my life here and now and appreciate all the effort that others have gone to, to make my world so interesting. I love knowing that I no longer have to live with all your old trophies, photographs and paintings. I can design and arrange my own living space, I can have a doona and choose my own doona covers for my bed, choose furniture for my lounge room, china for my kitchen and I can put flowers wherever I want.

There's an entire interior design universe waiting for me.

I can wear tracksuits and socks with toes around the house. I can wear bras with no underwire and let the girls out as soon as I get home. I can dress to please myself. I can wear warm nighties and dressing gowns and in time, I will be able to get new clothes that reflect the new me.

I can lie in bed making sheet angels. I can lie in the middle or diagonally and find a cool spot. I no longer have to avoid the wet spot. I can sleep in late. I can eat in bed. I can read in bed all day if I want to. There is such a glorious freedom in having a bed to myself. They say the one thing widows miss most is the sound of their husband snoring. I don't think I will have that problem. I won't have to try to get to sleep before you do so that I won't hear you snore like a steam train. I won't have to nudge you to turn over and I won't wait with bated breath to hear you breathe again. I won't wake up three times a night – every time you need to pee.

I gladly give all that to your girlfriend. She just can't have my house.

Please remember to have your sleep apnea test done, darling. I don't want to get news that you died in your sleep, not yet anyway – or maybe I do, no, just kidding, not really.

I can sing or whistle out loud without you telling me I can't hold a tune in a bucket and yelling at me to shut up, or to change the song (just because I have been singing the same one for a while). I will have the freedom to sing or whistle in my own home! I can play Dave Grusin's powerful soundtrack from 'The Firm', loud and long. Would I give up the opportunity of having a relationship with the love of my life for the chance to sing or whistle? The way I feel now, I would.

There's a whole musical universe waiting for me.

I never have to visit your family again or be nice to the ones I don't like. I don't have to do your parents' shopping, pay their bills or help with their housework. I will miss Amanda and I will be disappointed if she no longer wants to see me, but I am thrilled that I never have to spend Christmas with your Uncle George who always tried to kiss me on the mouth with tongue. *Why did you never tell me he did that?* I hear you ask. What would you have done? I reply.

I never have to buy presents for your mother who always found something wrong with whatever I chose, when she was just upset that I bought the present and you didn't. I gladly hand that over to your girlfriend. I can take my long service leave and not have to use it to go fishing or golfing with you. I've always thought of golf as a good walk ruined and now I'll never have to play golf again. I can go anywhere and do anything from December until March. I can write, I can travel, I can meet new people and learn new things.

There really is an entire, wonderful universe waiting for me.

Sam rang not long ago and asked for you. I told him you were out playing golf. I almost added, "with you", but that would have given the game away. You were allegedly on a golfing weekend with him. I think Sam called me because he knew about the alibi and he wanted me catch you out, but I didn't want to. I wasn't ready to take any action just yet.

Sam wanted to know if we could catch up over a cup of coffee. He had something he wanted to tell me. In all our married life, I have never met with any of your friends for coffee or for anything else and I wasn't about to start now. I told Sam that if he couldn't tell me over the phone, then I probably didn't need to know. He said that he admired me and reiterated that if I needed anything at all, I should call him. He said he would be available anytime. I thanked him, hung up the phone and thought, *not in a thousand years.*

A few days later, I received an anonymous letter. It said simply, "Your husband is having an affair with his assistant. I thought you should know." My gut instinct told me that Sam had sent it, but I couldn't be sure that your girlfriend hadn't. Maybe Sam wanted me to be unhappy and go running to him. Maybe your girlfriend wanted me to confront you and leave you. I considered the possibility that you had sent it and wanted the same thing. Maybe it was someone else entirely. Whatever they or you wanted, I wanted something else. I wasn't going to play that game so I put the letter in the bin. It didn't tell me anything I didn't already know. I watched you very closely that night but there was no change in you.

Last month, you told me you were going to a seminar on the weekend and I said, "Okay darling, no problems."

I felt mischievous and decided to have some fun.

"How about I come with you?" I asked. "I've got nothing planned this weekend. I would enjoy a weekend away with you." I just wanted to see the look of panic on your face.

"Just kidding," I said when I saw that look. "I know you will be too busy with…work to have time to keep me happy."

"Yes… I probably will be," you replied. You looked guilty and turned away to finish packing. There was a little hesitation in your voice, as though you might really have liked to take me with you, which pleased me.

That weekend, I went away by myself. I booked into a lovely hotel in the high country. I took long walks, and what surprised me was the extraordinary peace I found while walking on my own. I was alone but not lonely, I was not at all lonely. I went to galleries and craft shops, and I stopped and had cappuccinos and delicious lunches. I visited wineries and I went to the top of the mountains to see the view. I took my laptop with me and worked on my book and project in the evenings. I had time to look at things I had probably looked at all my life but never really seen. A kangaroo almost hit my car as it bounded out across the road. It touched the side of the car and reared up in fright. I looked at it in the rear-view mirror as it regained its balance, reached the other side of the road and disappeared from view.

I saw massive flocks of white cockatoos and listened to the beautiful call of currawongs. That weekend away was different from anything I had done in thirty years. I always had to consider whatever I did in terms of what you wanted and now, I didn't have to. I ate out for breakfast, lunch and dinner. I went to the movies alone for the first time in my entire life.

I looked at couples who were away for the weekend and it occurred to me that I might bump into the two of you, but that was a chance I was willing to take because the weekend away was so worth it.

I began to play with the idea of telling you that I was leaving you. I was beginning to feel as though the universe was paving the way for me. Everything felt easier. Everything that would have felt daunting or even impossible a short while ago, now felt like the next logical step. People I wanted to meet appeared, things that interested me showed up. The better it got, the better it got.

I mentioned it to Anne at our session in October and asked, "What is that?"

She smiled and said, "So you've noticed that the better it gets, the better it gets? How would you feel if you believed that no matter what was happening around you, you were attracting what you wanted and that things were always working out for you?"

"Wow, that would be amazing."

"Well, why not live as if you believed it?" she said. "Why not treat every negative event as just clarifying what you want and why?"

"Like a lesson?"

"No, there are no lessons, no karma, no punishments, no negative consequences from past life experiences. There are only clarifying events. If they feel negative, you can call them contrast, like the background in a painting that highlights the foreground so you can see it more clearly."

"That's a great way of looking at bad stuff that happens," I exclaimed. "I could just say to myself – that was some clarifying contrast."

"Then you could turn your attention to possible solutions and start a rampage of appreciation." said Anne.

"Rampage of appreciation?" I asked. That was such a weird term.

"A rampage of appreciation is a process for feeling better that I found in a book." said Anne. "It is when you think or write or talk aloud about something you love about your life, something you are sure of and you love knowing. It is the quickest way of moving yourself up the ladder. Try it sometime."

Chapter 25

The Best And The Rest

When I thought about what life might be like without you, a word popped up in my head that made me pause. I went for a walk to consider the possibility that I would lose more than I could ever possibly gain by leaving you. The word was lonely. Will I be lonely if we are not together? I wasn't lonely when I went away, but that was only a weekend. I was now thinking about the rest of my life. So, will I be lonely? I don't know yet. Maybe, but I do know that there is nothing lonelier than lying in bed next to the person you love most in the world, unable to say anything, believing that anything you say would blow your world apart. That's lonely.

So, no, I don't think I will be lonely. Will I ever re-marry or live with someone else? I don't know yet. Ask me one day when I meet someone who is not just after a nurse, purse, cook or housekeeper. Ask me then. I might know then, and if I don't meet anyone else, that's okay too.

About a month ago, I decided that I couldn't share a bed or have sex with you anymore. The idea that you had been in someone else recently became so revolting to me that I had to give it up. I used to think that I could compete with her. For a while, I even used my one-night stand as a 'highlight reel,' but that lost its power and I began to avoid having sex with you.

I saw a show on TV about AIDS, and where once I would have believed myself safe from it, I now felt a creeping horror that perhaps I wasn't. I used to think I knew who you slept with but that was no longer true and

I certainly didn't know who else your girlfriend had slept with. I also couldn't bear the thought that you might be thinking of her when you were with me. Do you remember the night when I couldn't let you in? That was the beginning of the end of it all for me. I couldn't bear the thought of you knowingly risking my safety and my life.

I told you the doctor said I was having a temporary severe reaction to menopause and that it would be over soon – one month, tops. I said that the night sweats and itching made me want to sleep in a bed by myself for a while. You looked both disappointed and relieved.

That first night in the spare room was difficult. I slept fitfully and thought of you alone in the bed where we had been together for so long. Over the next week or so I got used to it and began to sleep really well. I woke up each morning with the intention of being happy. I practiced my rampages of appreciation and I found lots of things to enjoy in my life.

Early last month, I greeted Anne with the news that I was leaving you, but that I still had hesitations and doubts about it. There was so much to leave for and so much to stay for. You were still the man I loved.

"Wait thirty days before you decide," said Anne. "Get happy, relax, make lists of positive aspects of your life and of him, do rampages of appreciation, do what you love doing and at the end of thirty days, if you still want to leave, then go. There is no right or wrong about staying or leaving, but be sure before you act. Don't go simply because you are still afraid to confront him. Examine all hesitations, all shifts in your emotions until the way is clear for you, whichever direction that is in, and if it's not a hell yeah, then it's a hell no!"

I balked at the idea of waiting another thirty days. I thought I had done enough lists. I was almost absolutely sure. I was almost ready.

"Almost isn't good enough," said Anne. "It's conflicted emotion, which can lead to regret. Decide when all your emotions are headed in the one direction. Decide only when you know you're floating downstream."

I waited the thirty days. I wrote in my journal and every time I thought about staying, I felt sad and discouraged. Every time I thought about leaving you, I felt relieved and happy. My mind was full of exciting plans and possibilities, projects and dreams. I had things I wanted to do. There were also things I knew I would miss. I finally wrote a list of what I would miss about you. It included many things, big and small. When I looked back at the list of things I would *not* miss about you, it was a much longer list, but all those things were trivial irritations. The things I would miss are not as tangible. How do I say that I will miss the love of my life?

I will miss watching your eyes shine when your beloved football team gets a goal. I loved it when you didn't want me to go with you to the matches because you didn't want to have to worry about whether or not I was having a good time. Isn't that odd, I loved it when you didn't want me there. I understood it.

I loved the way you understood when I needed my space too. I didn't want you around when I shaved my legs, when I talked with my friends or when I was curled up with a good book. Talking of good books, the Sandra Bullock character in the movie 'The Lake House' mentioned one of my absolute favorite books and movies, Jane Austen's 'Persuasion'. I made you watch that too and you remarked how the English actress Amanda Root could look plain and beautiful at the same time. I loved the way you noticed that. I thought she was like me, a small, plain, brown bird. I think it's also why I loved 'Jane Eyre' so much and why I could read it and watch it repeatedly. I will miss being your little brown bird, your BB.

I will miss your warm body in bed, the texture of your hands on my body, the hair on your chest that felt so great against my breasts. I have always loved the wrinkles at the side of your eyes when you smiled and the loving relationship you had with the kids. I have always loved the pained look on your face when you mowed the lawns, the many and varied ways you laughed when you were surprised, delighted or intrigued and your appalling delivery of jokes that made them all the funnier. I have always loved the wry way you patted your stomach when you knew you had eaten too much, and I will miss the distracted, noisy way you ate crunchy cereal.

I remember your attempt to grow a beard. It looked so much more like pubic hair than facial hair that the children and I begged you to shave it off. I remember your admiration and awe around Henry, how you looked at him as though you couldn't believe we had created something so equally impressive and challenging. That reminds me of the way Henry and Eleanor used to pluck cicada shells off the trees and stick them to their jumpers. They competed with each other to see who had the most and who had climbed the highest to get them. Do you remember how they would shriek with delight at the creepiness of it, knowing that they were just cicada shells, but never being entirely sure they wouldn't spring to life? Maybe cicada shells do have a purpose, after all.

Do you remember when we found huntsman spider bodies in the house but still couldn't pick them up with our bare hands for the same reason? Do you remember getting Henry over his fear of huntsmen when he was four? You encouraged him to name all the huntsmen with names like his so he could imagine they were friends coming to visit, and for the next few years, we had big, hairy Hugos, Humphreys, Henriettas and Hyacinths sitting in corners near the ceiling. We had a Harry Potter and a Hermione. We were under instruction from Henry to "Let them live their little lives." Maybe it was our huntsman strategy that turned him into such a defender of animal rights. I think we did a good job with Henry. We did a great job with both our kids.

I will miss our times at the bathroom basin in the evenings when we chatted about our day while we brushed our teeth. We could both feel the delicious tension of being in the mood and knowing that the rest of the evening would be delightful. I will miss all that about you and more, but I'm not grieving that it's gone. I can remember it any time I want to. In the meantime, I'm singing Kelly Clarkson's 'Breakaway'.

I had the very, very best of you, my darling Mike. She can have the rest of you.

Will she love those things about you? Will she find your habits endearing? I hope so, for your sake. Will she try to change you? Probably. I have already noticed some little changes. You (or she) bought new ties, in different colors. My husband, who always insisted that any tie was fine as long as it was blue, is now wearing yellow and red.

As I look back now, I realize with some shame that our lives were boring. I don't know why I struggled so hard to keep the status quo, to prevent change, when what I was trying to save was pleasant enough, but boring and repetitive. If you hadn't had an affair we might have been doing the same things until death. No dinky little holiday on a tropical island could compare to what I am doing now.

I am so happy where I am and so eager about pursuing my new life. I didn't feel that way before. My mind was taken up with the repetitive details of life: the job, your parents, grocery shopping, the laundry and gardening. My horizons were small and growing smaller by the minute. Now I feel my horizons expanding beyond anything I could have possibly imagined. I don't need you. I love you but I don't need you. I can manage my own finances, change a light bulb, have the car serviced and change a tire (well almost). I can survive and thrive.

Now I can sit alone in a restaurant and be perfectly content. That may not sound like much of an achievement, but it is. It really is.

Chapter 26

Twisting Rings Again

Every night for the past two weeks, I have come home from work, organized dinner and sat in the dining room, looking at my hands and twisting my rings. Every night I have told myself that this is the day I tell you I want you to leave. This is the day that I tell you I have a new life. *This* is the day that I tell you I want you gone. Every night I imagined a different scenario:

You begged me not to do this. You fell to your knees.

You told me you loved me.

You asked me if we could talk about it. You asked me why.

You made promises to change/improve/stop seeing her.

You burst into tears. You sobbed uncontrollably.

You threatened to kill me. You threatened to kill yourself.

You had a heart attack.

You threw things at me and screamed. You laughed hysterically.

You yelled good riddance.

You said, okay good, goodbye, I am going. My suitcase is packed. Get a solicitor.

However, no matter what you said or did, the outcome was always the same. I always left or made you leave. Then, every day, when you came in through the door, I got up and pretended I was busy doing something ordinary. Inside, I was seething with excitement. I was happy, and you felt that, I think. You seemed to want to be around even more. Our conversations were friendlier and more relaxed, but it was all too late, much too late. The ball was rolling downhill and gathering momentum.

Early last week, I got a call from a publisher, asking me to come in for an interview. He had looked at the material sent by the professor at the Institute and wanted to discuss publishing options, so I agreed to see him the following day. At first, I couldn't believe it. It was so exciting. Then, I did believe it. It was the next logical step toward my freedom. I wanted to jump up and hug myself, and then I wanted to hug you, Anne and Sue and the Eleanor and Henry. I wanted to hug Anita who transcribed my work and Ryan who took care of my computer stuff. I wanted to hug you the most, but I knew I couldn't let that happen. I could never let you know what I had been doing. You might talk me out of it. You might want part of it. You might want to take it away from me. You might decide you want to keep me now that I might be worth some money.

So I went into town and up to the eleventh floor of a fancy new building. There I was introduced to a man who took me to his office, sat me down, gave me coffee and told me that, from what he had read so far, my book 'had merit' and was 'eminently publishable'. The publisher explained that I would need to think about whether I wanted the book to be an e-book as well. My mind was beginning to buzz. Then he asked me what kind of advance I was hoping for from a publisher. Advance? My mind buzzed some more. He explained that an advance is part of a contract that gives him the exclusive right to publish the book on my behalf once it is finished.

"How much is an advance usually?" I asked.

"That depends on the book and on how well-known the author is. Yours would probably be about five thousand dollars. How does that sound?"

I laughed and told him that five thousand dollars sounded just fine. "Where do I sign?"

He laughed too. He had evidently met keen new authors before. He took his check book out of his desk drawer and when I looked at it, another thought occurred to me.

"Could you please date it December 12?" I asked.

It was the day I would be leaving you.

The publisher handed me the check and I jumped up, walked around his desk and hugged him. We talked at length about deadlines, marketing processes and technical details. It was all so new and interesting to me. The publisher asked me if I had any other writing projects that may need publishing in the future. I mentioned my project to him, and he asked me to get it to him as soon as it was done. I left his office later that day, floating on air.

I couldn't wait to tell someone. I couldn't wait to tell you. Oh, my darling Mike, it was so exciting and I wanted to tell you about it so much. I wanted you to laugh and hug me and tell me that I was amazing and that my book was incredible, but at the time, I couldn't, so I called Sue. She squealed with delight. She was truly happy for me and I was happy for myself. To celebrate, I went out and bought myself some beautiful clothes. I spent nearly four hundred dollars on lingerie, a new dress, shoes and a bag, and a very nice afternoon tea. I don't know why. It seemed like the logical thing to do and it was so much fun.

I had to tell someone else my news so when I got home, I called the kids. I called Sue again, I called Anne and left a message on her answering machine, and then I called Anita and Ryan. By the time you came home, I was humming with joy, but not needing to share it with you. That night you were home early and we had dinner out on the patio. It was a beautiful evening and dandelions were glowing in the early evening light. We sat and talked about nothing in particular. We talked tentatively on safe subjects like our kids, your work and mine. It felt to me like we were finding our way back to each other, slowly and carefully. It was an odd sensation, and it was both very nice and very, very troubling.

Would I have written a book if you hadn't had an affair? Would I have been able to leave you if I hadn't written the book? I think I might have, but it would have taken a lot longer and it would have been much harder.

I never thought I would ever be thanking you for having an affair, but here I am, doing just that.

Chapter 27

Choosing Happiness

Two nights before you left for the annual real estate conference, we had our last dinner together. Eleanor and Henry came over and I asked them to say nothing. I wanted us to have dinner together so I could pretend one last time that we were still a happy family. I made your favorite dinner. The kids thought they were coming over to watch their family implode. Even Henry looked anxious at first, but you and I were so relaxed with each other that he and Eleanor were relieved. You and Henry talked on the patio while Eleanor and I prepared dinner.

Eleanor was surprised that you and I looked so happy together. When we were in the kitchen getting the dessert, she asked me in a whisper, "Are you still going?"

"Yes," I replied. "I am definitely still going."

She looked doubtfully at me and. I shrugged.

"It's too little, too late," I said. I hugged her. "I will be okay," I whispered in her ear. "We will all be okay. I love you, blossom possum."

"I love you too, Mum. I hope you will be happy."

"I intend to be." I smiled at her and we went outside, bearing your favorite dessert – apple pie and cream. You looked relaxed too, as though you had come to an important decision and you were glad. The evening went well and we were a happy family again for a few short hours.

The following day was your company's Christmas cocktail party. You asked me to be there and I was surprised you even mentioned it. After all, your girlfriend would be there. I wore my new dress and I was feeling good, not beautiful, but good. I arrived at the function center and stood just inside the door. I saw her standing near you. She was dressed in emerald green. I noticed that when you moved around the room to talk to people, she followed you and spoke with the people you spoke to. She looked like she knew what you were talking about. She looked like your partner. I had no idea about real estate, I was there simply as your wife. It occurred to me that maybe you didn't need a little brown bird anymore. Maybe you needed a bright green parrot with orange claws. Your girlfriend looked like she belonged with you, but I wasn't ready to give her that satisfaction just yet.

I moved on in. I touched her on the arm and said, "Hi! It's so nice to see you again. How are you?" She looked disconcerted and uncomfortable, and so did you. She glanced anxiously at you and you looked away. It was then I realized that she hadn't told you she had come to our house, and you hadn't told her that you knew. Oh, what webs we weave, so many secrets and lies. The situation was awkward but eased by a waiter carrying glasses of champagne on a tray. I took one gratefully. I stood by you, and between you and her. I smiled up at you, then kissed you on the cheek and said, "Hi darling." This time she was the one to look away.

You took me across the room away from her and introduced me to people. I looked back to see her looking stranded and resentful, and for the second time, I almost felt sorry for her. Maybe things hadn't been going well between the two of you recently. You had been home so much more and we had been so much happier. Maybe she thought she had lost the battle or maybe she had just considered herself the hostess of the event. She probably had, and now I had taken what she thought was hers.

I was now the boss's partner, not her, and she looked a little dazed. I kept an eye on her in the distance while I spoke to other people. Then I saw Sam. His wife was flirting with a waiter somewhere and he looked lost. I went over to him and shook his hand.

"You are looking especially lovely tonight," he said, looking deeply into my eyes and holding my hand in a firm grip.

"Thanks Sam. I can always rely on you to make me feel better." I smiled back at him.

He leaned towards me and said. "I would like to be able to do that more often. He doesn't deserve you, you know."

I smiled at him, looked across at your girlfriend, looked back at him, winked and said, "Yes, I know he doesn't, but then, neither do you." I withdrew my hand and walked back to you. I thought, *not in a million years.*

I enjoyed standing with you, belonging to you and seeing the respect in the eyes of those you spoke to, but after a short while it began to pall. I was bored and restless. I had better things to do. I had a book and a project to finish. This wasn't my world and I really wasn't interested in your networking or your business deals.

I went to the Ladies and when I came out of the stall, I saw your girlfriend's reflection in the mirror, looking at mine. I wasn't nervous, just curious to see what she would say or do. Her eyes were brimming with tears and for the first time, she looked young and vulnerable. She was pretending to fix her eye make-up with a tissue.

She smiled tentatively at me.

"Have a good time in Perth," she said, in an attempt to sound cheerful.

That took me by surprise. I had assumed you were taking her with you.

"Oh, I am not going!" I replied.

"Really?" She looked startled and dismayed.

"Really," I said. "Maybe he is taking someone else. We both know he cheats."

I was tempted to be cruel, but she looked so shocked and miserable that I took pity on her.

"I have no idea about his plans," I said.

"He told me yesterday he wasn't taking me. I've lost him, haven't I?" she said, more as a statement than a question.

I took a deep breath and looked at her reflection intently. The time for pretending was over. There were so many mean things I could have said to her, so many things that once I would have enjoyed saying to her. I could have said yes, you stupid fat cow, you have lost him. You never really had him, he was always mine and you deserve to be miserable. You knew he was married when you started sleeping with him. You knew he was a liar and an adulterer because he was cheating with you and lying to me. You met me and you knew I loved him, yet you kept seeing him – but he is mine. You saw him tonight. He loves me…

On the other hand, I could have said, no actually, I don't want him anymore. I am leaving him tomorrow. I am leaving him to you. He's all yours… but I didn't want her to know in case she said something to you. I wanted to get out of there quickly, so the option I went with was:

"You haven't lost him yet. Be patient just a little longer."

She stared at me. "What do you mean?"

"Wait, just wait." I whispered.

Why did I say that? I can't really tell you for sure, Mike. Suddenly there just didn't seem to be any reason to continue the fight or to prove anything. There was no point at all in being mean to her, and given what I was going to do to you the very next day, I didn't want to. I wanted to leave with as little on my conscience as possible. Maybe I just didn't want to leave you with absolutely nobody or nothing at all.

"I do love him, you know." Her voice broke a little.

For the first time, I really did feel sorry for her. I no longer saw her just as the source of my pain. I saw her as someone who, under different circumstances, I might have liked. I also saw her as my ticket to freedom. If you still had her, you might find it easier to let me go. I paused and looked at her directly for the first time.

"Yes, I can see that. We had that in common, I loved him too," I replied. She looked surprised as I gently touched her arm and walked quickly back out to you.

Once I found you in the crowd, I stayed with you, talked to people and drank champagne. You kept me by your side for the remainder of the evening. When I tried to move away, you held my hand. You introduced me to everyone. You looked lovingly at me, but I mistrusted you. I told myself that this was all for show, just like your birthday party. Later, I saw you looking at something on the other side of the room so I looked in the same direction. She was standing there, staring at us. I smiled briefly at her and looked at you. Your facial expression was a complicated mixture of love and regret. She looked at me one last time, then moved towards the exit and was gone. I didn't know her name and now I didn't need to. I could forget her completely.

Eventually everyone left and the caterers started to clean up. I waited for you to turn your back on me again, the way you did after your speech at your birthday party. I waited to see if your performance was just for show. But when we drove home, you reached over, took my hand and placed it on your thigh, and held it there.

"Thank you for coming tonight," you said.

"I enjoyed it," I replied, which was almost true.

"Come with me, BB," you said.

"Where?"

My heart began to hammer. You hadn't used my nickname for such a long time.

"Come to Perth with me. We could have fun when I am not working. You could relax and enjoy yourself at the spa. You would just have to take tomorrow and Monday off work."

For a minute, I held my breath. Your affection at the cocktail party wasn't all for show. My world turned over and I thought I had made a terrible mistake. My plans were going to take effect the very next day. Your affection *wasn't* all for show. I had won you back. Everything that I had been working toward, everything I had wanted for the past ten months was within reach. That tiny corner of hope was still there. You were coming back to me. You were mine again.

If I wanted to, I could pretend that your affair had never happened. I could take two days off and go with you. I could be with you. You would be mine again, always.

My voice choked on a sob and I couldn't speak.

"Are you all right, my darling?" you asked.

"Yes," I said softly. "I'm okay."

"You have been so distant lately," you said. "You have been happy, distracted and somewhere else. I thought I was losing you. I thought that maybe you had met somebody else."

I looked at you and said, "I am sorry. No, there is nobody else." How ironic.

"We will be okay, BB. We are okay," you said. You squeezed my hand. "Come to Perth with me, tomorrow."

I hesitated. Part of me wanted to shout, Yes! Yes! I wanted to go home and pack for a four-day holiday with you. Another part of me wanted to follow my dreams. I needed time to think. I had to make a decision that was to affect my life forever and I needed more time to think.

"I would really love to; let me think," I said. I sat quietly for a while and nobody looking at me could possibly have imagined the turmoil I was in. Stay with you or leave you? I sat there, my hand on your thigh, your hand covering mine, and asked myself if I could undo everything that I had set in motion. I felt guilty, because I knew what was going to happen the following day. That trip home was the most confused and complicated time of my life. You loved me and you had chosen me. I could choose you and undo everything else. I could step back into my life and go on as before. All I had to do was make one phone call in the morning - one little phone call - and I seriously considered it. I almost confessed to you, but the words wouldn't come. I am very glad now that I said nothing. This story would have had a very different ending, and I like the one it has.

"I am sorry, Mike," I said, "but I have to interview applicants on both days. All the appointments are booked." I looked at you regretfully. "I can't come tomorrow, but I am glad you asked." You glanced quickly at me with the most loving smile.

When we arrived home from the cocktail party, you asked me to move back into our bedroom and I did. We made love again. It was tender and passionate and there was no need for highlight reels. We made love for the last time; only you didn't know it was the last time.

Afterward, I lay awake for hours. I wished there were two of me, one who would stay with you and lie in your arms at night, and the other who would embark on the adventure. Then when I asked myself which one of those two I would like to be, I knew that I wanted to be the one who flew away to freedom. I couldn't turn back. Forms were signed, tickets were bought, plans had been made and instructions had been given. Dreams were coming true, adventures were beginning and horizons were expanding. I didn't want to turn back now.

I had discovered the thrill of deciding what I wanted to do. I was no longer living according to the role I happened to be playing: wife, manager, mother or friend. I was no longer going to get up at the same time, make the same breakfast and do the housework in the same order that I had always done it. You would not be with me, wasting my time, slowing me down with your need for dinners or company in front of the television. I couldn't be content with what I had before. I couldn't slot myself back into that life. I had created a fascinating future and it was waiting for me. All I had to do was claim it.

I had discovered that I couldn't appreciate happiness unless I could choose it. It is the choosing and the focus that makes it so delicious. Now, I want to explore that happiness. I want to know what it would be like to travel, to live in an apartment, to be a published, best-selling author and so much more, and I can't do that with you. I can't imagine you being able to step up and be what I want now. In spite of your running around with that woman, you're winding down. You like quiet evenings, and I am revving up. You sit on the couch and I want to be out in the world. I don't want to drag you kicking and screaming into my new world. It's my new world precisely because you're not in it. Is that selfish? I hope so. It's about time.

So where am I going when I leave you? I won't tell you, simply because I don't want to. I am now living my life based on the principles that there is nothing more important than feeling good and that life is supposed to be fun. My joy list is the longest list I have ever written.

When I leave you, I will be in either a small villa tucked away in the south of France, an infinity pool at a resort in Hawaii, a country cottage in Devon, on a cruise in Alaska, staying at El Questro resort in Western Australia, or all of the above. You get the general idea. After that? I'll see what inspires me. I might learn Italian in Italy or Spanish in Spain. I might learn to ride a horse, I might take French cookery classes, I might go white water rafting on the Colorado River or ski the long slopes in Utah. I might hike across Milford Sound in New Zealand, learn the samba, the cha-cha, yoga, tai-chi or Pilates. I might walk the Pilgrimage of St James. I might visit Pamplona and watch the running of the bulls, or see the Mayan ruins in Peru.

I might snorkel the Great Barrier Reef or see the terracotta warriors in China. I might write several more books. I might work in an orphanage, I might settle somewhere warm in Australia and have the kids (and future grandchildren) visit and stay as long as they like. I might create a business and establish a charity with the profits, I might do wine-tasting tours, trekking tours or hot air ballooning. Ooh, ooh, ooh, Snorkeling! Surfing! Para-sailing! Scuba-diving!

When I get back from this first adventure, I am going to work as much or as little as I like. I will see Eleanor and Henry regularly and maybe I will take them with me on a holiday of their choice.

One thing I do know for sure, Mike, is that I am going to be a truly happy woman. I am going to remember you with fondness and maybe I will think about you at least ten times a day for the rest of my life – or not.

Now at this point, I imagine you are feeling a bit panicked about how my leaving will affect you. Speaking legally, here is what your solicitor friend told me. Mum left the house to the Eleanor and Henry so we have no legal right to it and they have the right to sell it whenever they want. You have your business and your pension plan; I have my job and my pension plan. I won't touch yours if you don't touch mine.

Please don't waste your time trying to contest my mother's will. Just let it go. You would lose more in solicitors' fees and the kids' love than you would ever gain. Besides, I don't have as much money saved as you do because I took time off to have children, so you will get out of this quite well. You just don't own a house, or even half a house. If it makes you feel any better, neither do I. Also, don't try to find out where I am now or where I will be living. The kids have promised me they won't tell you.

How can you do any or all of that? I hear you ask. I'll tell you later. My options are endless. My only criteria will be: Will I like it, will it be easy, will it be fun, and is it selfish? I do know one thing. I won't be going anywhere we've been together. I'm not going over old ground. *Will you do all this alone?* I hear you ask. Maybe, maybe not, I don't know yet. I'll figure it out as I go along. *How can you afford to do all or any of this?* Because I know something you don't, I reply with a smile.

Do I ever wish I had said something to you at the very beginning? Sometimes I do. But now that I am happy, would I wish for a different kind of happiness? Given who I was back then, I couldn't have done anything differently, so I am where I am now and I am at peace with that and eager for more. Not more of the same, I am eager for more of different, more of new, more of exciting, interesting, liberating, clarifying and joyful. I am ready and eager for an adventure, which is why I am leaving you.

If it doesn't work out between you and your girlfriend, do I want you to call me? Do I want to leave that door open? No, I don't. If you have already decided that you don't want her, guess what, it's too late. This bird has flown and she isn't flying back. I can't go back. I don't want to go back. Going back and repairing my relationship with you would be like cleaning out old pipes, which would be too much like hard work. I have decided to do what is easier and more fun. I am going to lay new pipes.

The kids approve. In fact, they're cheering from the sidelines.

Chapter 28

On The Runway

Last Friday was December 7. You packed for your Perth conference while I pretended to get ready for work. I had the feeling you would have stayed at home if I had asked you to. You dropped hints about the distance and the cost. But I didn't ask; I didn't want you to stay home. By going to Perth, you were giving me the opportunity to make my break.

You were finally ready to go. I carried your briefcase to the front door and you put your suitcase down. You enfolded me in a hug and for the second time in our relationship, you let go after me. When you picked up your briefcase and suitcase, I kissed you goodbye like it was an ordinary day and you were just heading off on a short business trip. But it would be the last time I might see you, possibly for years, so I took a mental photo of you as you left. I couldn't go out and see you off because it wouldn't seem normal, and you might become suspicious. I was anxious for you to be gone, so I could be gone too.

"See you Tuesday night after I get a few things done at the office," you said. "I will miss you." You kissed me again.

I looked at you and said nothing. There was nothing more to be said, I wanted to remember this image of you always, so I just smiled – and then you were gone.

Once the door shut behind you, I leaned against it. The decision was made and there was no turning back. It was done. I felt shaky, but good. There was no hesitation and there were no regrets. All my energy was now going in one direction. I went upstairs and pulled out the hidden boxes that were already packed and I started to pack what was remaining. Sue came over to help and we packed china, cutlery, clothes and linen. We assembled cardboard boxes and put either my name, your name, or the kids' names on them. We put red and blue stickers on the furniture. The blue stickers were for you, the red were for Eleanor and Henry to decide between them and the few unmarked pieces of furniture was mine. I wanted to take very little with me. Sue and I had fun. We put on our favorite music and drank lots of coffee.

The song 'Walking on Sunshine' came on and I sang along. I danced around and laughed at the memory of The Big Bang Theory's comic bookstore owner, Stuart, naked but for one towel around his waist and another turbaned on his head, singing it in karaoke. By the way, I am keeping one other memento from our time together. I am keeping the 'Knock-Knock Penny Knock-Knock Penny' mug that I gave you for your birthday last year. I really like that mug and when I use it, I will think of the happy times we had.

Eleanor and Henry came over too. They wanted to be part of the process and to take what was important to them. They packed their favorite things: plates they had decorated in kindergarten, mugs with their names on them, photo albums, books and little things that reminded them of their childhood. They took photos of the house and the garden. Henry called the photos his 'before shots'. They talked loudly and happily to each other while they worked and I was happy to have them there. I could see they liked Sue and she liked them. I helped the kids carry their things to their cars and hugged them.

The removal van arrived. The workers loaded everything with your name or a blue sticker on it and took it away. Then they came back with the storage key and took my boxes and furniture to my new apartment. Finally, the house was completely empty. Sue and I walked around to check that everything was done. I sat with her for a while on the patio, exhausted, happy and sad all at the same time. She hugged me and left. I was finally alone.

The last thing I took down was the kitchen pin board, all its photos, old decorations, school reports, timetables and scraps of paper, all the little reminders of a life I was leaving behind. I put all the papers into a shoe box, took one last look around the house, locked the front door behind me, turned off the electricity at the meter and the water at the front tap. I picked a dandelion and pressed it flat into my wallet, got into my car and drove away. Our telephone account has been cancelled and paid for and your mail has been redirected to a post office box, which explains the other key.

Now, it is time to tell you what I have done, darling! Two months ago, the day after Eleanor told me that she needed me to make a decision quickly, we went to a real estate agent with Henry to put the house on the market. There was a specific condition on the sale. It had to be sold to someone who was prepared to pull the house down within three days of the settlement date. Yes, you read right. It had to be pulled down.

"Are you serious?" the agent asked. "Isn't it enough just to sell it? It's a good house in one of the most sought-after suburbs in Melbourne. People will pay top dollar for the location alone."

"It's a great house," I said, "but it's also an old house that probably needs a new roof and new wiring, built-in wardrobes, a pantry, an ensuite bathroom and all the other things that people think they need these days. I want it pulled down. That's the condition, and there's no debate. I have my reasons, I want it pulled down and I want you to get me a price worthy of the location."

The agent looked from me to Eleanor and Henry and they nodded.

The agent soon called to say that he had a buyer, and the house was sold four weeks ago. The settlement date was the day you left for your annual conference and the demolition day was to be the following day. It was so much easier than we thought it would be. Eleanor and Henry were happy to think about their student loans disappearing and having money in the bank. Eleanor intends to use hers for a deposit on an apartment of her own and Henry wants to keep his for future studies. At the same time, the agent found me a nice, small apartment, not far from where we lived, which Eleanor and Henry now own. It is perfect for right now. It is as much as I need and nothing I can't leave behind at a moment's notice. No pot plants, no pets. It's my definition of total freedom.

How could you! That was my home too, as much as it was yours! I hear you say. Nuh-uh! I reply. We paid a peppercorn rent for twenty-six years, since our wedding day. You had an easy ride and now it's over. *You didn't leave me with much!* I hear you say. Yes I did. You still have a perfectly good suitcase, a little battered perhaps, but still serviceable. I am just kidding, Mike. There are enough things in the storage unit for you to start again. I didn't touch your credit card; I am not that mean. You still have your girlfriend. You still have your work and I won't go for your savings unless you try to go for anything that belongs to me or the kids. Besides, you're an estate agent; you know the ropes, so find yourself something. Just don't come anywhere near me. My solicitor will get the divorce papers to you in due course.

But I have nowhere to go! I hear you say. Yes you do, I reply. If your girlfriend loves you, she will have you at her place. It's not my problem. *But I don't want to live with her! I chose you! I came back to you!* Too late, my darling, way, way too late. Perhaps you had better tell her that you left me and not the other way around. She may not want you if she thinks I dumped you.

Why did you do it this way? I hear you ask. Because it was the only way I could protect me and mine. I had to get in before you. *You could have just sold it!* Nuh-uh! You might have bought it and there was *no way on this earth* I was going to let that woman move into my home. She might have had children. She might have lived my life. No way was I ever going to let that happen. The only way to ensure she couldn't was to make sure there was nothing for you to buy. Be grateful; she still loves you and she might still love you now that you are homeless.

Where are you going? I hear you ask. What's it to you? I reply. *But you're my wife!* No, I'm not your anything anymore. I understand that this is a shock to you. You thought you had everything under control. You thought you had got away with what you were doing, but you didn't. Now, you'll just have to build a bridge and get over it. *Why didn't you say something*? I hear you ask. *I wish you had. I might have fought to keep you. You never gave me a chance to fight for you.*

I did say something. Every time I asked you how you were, every time I asked you if everything was all right, if we were okay, every time I hugged you, every meal I made, every birthday party I organized, every time we made love, every word I said every day – you chose to ignore it all. Why didn't *you* say anything? I gave you many chances. Why didn't you take them?

But I love you! I hear you say. Not enough, not nearly enough, I reply.

Later that day, I met Eleanor and Henry at the solicitor's office where the divorce papers were signed and my new will was finalized. We went to the estate agent and met the buyer. The papers for the house were signed. The buyer was a nice man, about my age. He had a set of architect's drawings of the house he planned to build on our block of land. He reminded me of the Steve Martin character in 'It's Complicated'. He appeared gentle, intelligent and unassuming, and I liked him.

"Are you free to have a coffee?" he asked. "I'd like to show you my plans. I want you to know that I won't be building units or a monster on your land."

"Yes, she is free," said Eleanor, giving me a smile and a wink. "See you later, Mum." She and Henry headed off to deposit the bank check.

The buyer and I went to a nearby coffee shop and settled into a corner table. He rolled out his plans. I enjoyed listening to him talk about his new house. He asked me for a woman's point of view and I told him that no one wants to wash dishes while they look at a wall. I suggested he widen the kitchen bench at the sink and enlarge the kitchen window so that there would be room to put flower pots between the sink and the glass. He thought that was a good idea.

"Why did you want your house pulled down? To destroy memories?" he asked.

"No," I said, "to preserve them. Why are you building a new home?"

"To create memories."

"A good reason," I said.

We talked for a while about his plans and mine. It felt good.

"Call me tomorrow when my house is ready to go," I said as I gave him my number and got up to leave.

The next day, when I received the phone call from the buyer, Eleanor, Henry and I drove to our street, parked across the road from our house, and got out of the car. The buyer was talking to a man in a hard hat. I joined them and had a quick chat with the hard hat man. A big machine was poised in front of my house, ready to tear it down. The buyer, the kids and I leaned against my car and watched my beautiful home disappear forever. Henry and the buyer took photos. When I found it difficult to watch, the buyer put his arm around my shoulders. The demolition happened so quickly. The big bulldozer and wrecking crew had it all down in thirty minutes, except for one small detail. It took a little longer for the dust to settle, and then the trucks moved in.

I was glad the buyer was there with me. I enjoyed being part of the creation of his new home. He gave me his number and asked me to call him when I got back from my travels.

"I'd love you to see the progress I make on my house," he said.

"I just might do that," I said, lightly.

"I hope you do," he said.

When we said goodbye, he took my hand and held it.

I really would have enjoyed hiding somewhere and watching you arrive home today, to see you get out of the car and then become aware that you were looking at nothing – no house, no home, nothing but the three bottom steps remaining from the stairs to the front door, with a small, battered, brown suitcase perched on the top step. Other than that, just an empty block of land with trees around the edges. That would have been so good to see, but maybe nothing could be better than the way I have imagined it. Besides, I no longer care very much about how you feel. I care much more about how I feel and I want to feel great.

Since then, I have settled into my new home and visited the kids. We celebrated the end of their student loans and the beginning of my new life. Over the weekend, I worked on this letter to you and my other project. Last night, we celebrated Christmas. It was very different from all our other Christmases, but we all agreed that it was good anyway and that future ones would be better.

What I want now is to be able to feel comfortable when I see you at family events like weddings, births and funerals. We will always have a relationship and I want ours to be parked in a good place with no hostility or tension, no anger or embarrassment. I want it to be easy between us. I even want it to be easy between me and your girlfriend or second wife, whoever she may be. I am leaving all our mutual friends to you. They are your friends so tell them not to keep me informed. I don't want to know. You can introduce your girlfriend to them, if you haven't already, and good luck with that.

Say goodbye to your parents for me. I wish I could have, but it was too hard. When I saw them last Wednesday, I mentioned that you would be taking care of them the following week, as I had to take a short trip. I took the risk that they might mention it to you before I could make my escape, but as you called them so seldom, I thought the risk worth taking. If they had told you, I would have said I had a meeting I couldn't get out of. I hugged them both and told them I would see them soon, which wasn't strictly true, but it was the best I could do. After leaving them, I sat in my car and cried. I was part of their family for thirty years, and I loved them too. Leaving you meant losing them, particularly your father who is such a gentle soul.

Please tell them that I will be away for a few months and I will come to visit them (if they want me to) when I get back. I abdicate all responsibility for their care. That is something, as much as I love them, I gladly hand back to you. You will need to call them once a week, do their shopping, monitor their medication, spend time with them, supervise a cleaner and find nursing homes for them when the time comes. Maybe your girlfriend will do all that for you. If so then I gladly leave it to her.

Call Amanda and explain. Call Eleanor and Henry. They love you and they want to hear from you. It's up to you.

Chapter 29

Taking Flight

Today is December 12, 2012, the first anniversary of my mother's death, a good day for starting my new life.

Early this morning, I saw Anne for the last time. I had waited the thirty days, I did my lists of positive aspects about you and our life together, and another list of the positive aspects of what my life would be like without you. I told her that I had listened to my feelings and had felt enormous relief and excitement about the possibility of laying new pipes in a foundation for a new life, and I was practicing rampages of appreciation.

I told her that staying with you would have felt like a burdensome task, it would be cleaning out old pipes, trying to resurrect respect for you and trying to fit into an old framework. It sounded like hard work, like trying to repair something that was very badly broken. Whereas, when I thought about a different life somewhere else, it felt like I had jumped out of the well, I was floating downstream and I was laying new pipes. I told Anne that I could mix my metaphors as well as she could, and we laughed.

"Be light about this," said Anne. "Be happy about it. Don't feel that you need to defend, explain or justify your decision to me or to Michael or to anyone. Now that you have made that decision, go with it. This is your life."

I told Anne that my long service leave started today and I would be gone for some time. She said the twelfth of the twelfth was a good day to start a new life, whatever and wherever that is. When I mentioned it was also the anniversary of my mother's death, she suggested I get happy and talk to my mother, to let her in on my plans and listen for ideas.

"If you're miserable, you can't hear her," she said. "Get happy and watch for signs that she is around. Talk to her and to your father about what you are doing. Let them enjoy your enjoyment."

I told Anne that I would take the three months of long service leave to do some of what I have imagined and to finish my childcare book. I would call her when I got back and let her know how I am doing. She replied, "My door will always be open." I felt a faint pain in my heart at the thought of maybe never seeing her again, but I also knew that her words would always go with me, so in a sense I will always be able to talk to her. I can also refer back to these notes that I am writing to you and to the recordings I have made.

So Anne and I said goodbye for now and she reassured me that she would be happy to see me if I felt I needed any more fine-tuning. I said that I would always need fine-tuning because I would never be perfect, and she replied that this was a good thing, because perfection equals endedness.

"Go follow your bliss," she said.

Chapter 30

This Bird Has Flown

Later this morning, I had coffee with my old friends. We met at a coffee shop and they all shared their latest news. I sat and looked at them, feeling none of the previous familiarity or fondness. They were four strangers. They no longer knew anything about me and I was no longer the slightest bit interested in knowing anything about them. I could finally be brave enough to tell them what was going on and not care what they thought. I no longer had to be friends with them, and I could let them go. They were part of my past, but they would not be part of my future.

"Girls," I said. "I am leaving Michael today," I beamed. I sat back and watched their reactions. They looked at me like I had said I was bearing an alien's baby. I waited. Then they all spoke together.

"But you can't!"

"But I am," I said, smiling.

I saw two of them look sideways at each other and I guessed they already knew something. Their look of shock was not genuine. Their expressions said, *we think we should pretend we didn't know anything, but we really do want you and the others to see that we did.*

I looked across to the other two and saw innocent shock in their eyes. They were stunned. Obviously, they hadn't known. They were also horrified that they hadn't been told. I didn't want to be there when the fall-out occurred. Suddenly, they all began to ask questions at the same time, predictable questions that I was ready for. I remembered Anne's words: there was no need to justify, defend or explain.

"Why didn't you tell us?" they asked. "What happened, when, where, why, how?" "What are you going to do, where are you going?" "Do you have a boyfriend?" "A girlfriend?" "Does he have a boyfriend, a girlfriend, why didn't you tell us?"

I looked at each of them in turn and knew what would happen when I left, but I wasn't planning on seeing them again after today, so I didn't care. I was leaving them behind as I was leaving you behind, so I didn't care if two of them had known. I didn't care what their reasons were for not telling me what they knew, and I wasn't worried about what they would say behind my back the second I was gone. I was just pleased to be able to say simply, "I have decided to leave Michael. I am very happy about the decision and I am off now."

I put five dollars on the table for my coffee and got up to leave. They called after me, so I turned to say goodbye. I made no promises to meet them again.

Next, I went to the bank and deposited my publisher's check, my going-away present to myself. I love being able to say 'my publisher'! I bought some foreign currency. I bought a mobile phone with a new number.

All is well. The kids are taken care of. I have money in the bank. I have work in my future. I have one, maybe two, maybe more, published books in my future. I may have another newly-discovered, very lovable possibility in my future as well. I went to the travel agent to pick up my documents.

Now, finally, I am in my new home, ready to leave.

I have a plane to catch. Sue is driving me to the airport and it will be nice to have someone there to say goodbye and wish me bon voyage. I have a beautiful golden dandelion pinned to my jacket. By the time you get to the end of this letter, if you ever do, I will be long gone. This little brown bird has flown. In fact, I am not going to think of myself as a little brown bird anymore. I don't know what I am.

Maybe I am a dandelion. Maybe I can think of myself as something that springs up again after being mown down and my seed heads as ideas that will float around the world. What am I looking forward to now? Everything. I won't have to think about you and your girlfriend anymore. Won't that be lovely! Leaving you is a selfish decision that feels good. In fact, it feels great. It feels like "Hell, Yeah!"

Ten months ago, I put my boat into the stream and paddled against the current until I was exhausted. Then, I stopped paddling, the current turned my boat and I floated downstream. Now my stream has reached the ocean and it is time for me to catch my wave.

I wish you well.

With much love and gratitude for the past thirty years,

Katharine

PS: Merry Christmas.

PPS: My project is finished now. An amended copy of this manuscript is on its way to my publisher today, as an attachment to an email; names and details have been changed to protect the innocent. It is a novel called 'The Dandelion'. If it is a great success and is made into a movie, I want somebody fabulous, like Sandra Bullock, to play me."

Dear Reader,

This is where my letter to Michael ends. I don't know if he read it, but I like to believe he did.

Chapter 31

Six Months Later

Hello Reader,

You may be wondering what I did between 12 December and the end of February. I walked the Camino. It was winter in Spain and cold, but I walked 500 miles from a little town in France with the glorious name of St. Jean Pied de Port, over the Pyrenees, across Spain to a town with an even more glorious name and cathedral, Santiago de Compostela. It is believed by the faithful to be the final resting place of the disciple James, who fled his home after the crucifixion of Jesus.

On the way, I lay two beautiful stones on a small hill with a cross on top, in remembrance of my parents. I walked alone for the most part, and spent evenings with many wonderful people who I believe will become lifelong friends. I spent five weeks on the walk and celebrated Christmas in Pamplona. There was a comforting solitude spending Christmas with other pilgrims who were also walking the Camino and were far from the ones they loved.

While I walked, I cleared my head. I made plans and sang songs. I talked with people and admired the Spanish countryside, small villages and towns. After the Camino, I rented a small villa near the coast, where I could relax and keep working on my book. When it was as finished as I could make it, I sent it to my publisher.

I also wrote a letter of resignation to the childcare center. I recommended my assistant for my position and I hope they gave it to her. Then I flew to London and walked from there to Stratford Upon Avon. I had a joyous time, walking through villages that were settings for the TV series Midsomer Murders. It was a silly thing to do, but fun.

Finally, it was time to come home to my apartment and start work as a lecturer. My books were ready to be launched and I was busy and very happy.

One Saturday morning, not long after my return, I was sitting at the kitchen bench, looking at my pin board with all its new memories, and the name and telephone number of the buyer. The phone rang. It was Eleanor.

"Hi Mum," she said. "Just a quick call. I want to tell you something and ask you something. Which first?"

"Tell me something."

Eleanor took a deep breath. "Dad's girlfriend is pregnant."

I paused, to take in the information and to see how I felt.

"Mum? How are you feeling?"

"You know what, possum? I am just glad it's not me."

Eleanor and I laughed together.

"Yeah," she added. "I've spoken to Dad and he doesn't seem that thrilled…"

I cut her off. I didn't want to know.

"Next. What did you want to ask me?"

"Have you called him yet?"

"Him who?" I knew who she meant but I was stalling.

"Mum! You know who I mean. The buyer!"

I looked up at the pin board and touched the small, faded piece of paper pinned up there. His name was Andy.

"No, I haven't," I said. "He's probably forgotten me. He's probably married by now."

"Mum! I saw the way he looked at you. There is no way he could have forgotten you. Just call him, for God's sake!"

"Okay, I will, okay."

"When?"

"I will, I promise. Okay, I have to go, see you on Wednesday for dinner. Love you, bye."

Eleanor's mention of the buyer unsettled me. I had thought of him from time to time, his intense gaze, the way he held my hand. When we met, he made me feel both precious and shy, like an awkward teenager. I shook myself off, picked up my shopping bag and headed out to the street.

An hour later, with groceries in my bag, I walked along the street, looking for a place to stop for a coffee. I looked ahead and saw Andy walking toward me. He hadn't seen me yet, and when he did, I saw the sharp intake of breath that he took. I walked toward him and held out my hand to him. He took it and held it in both his hands. Immediately, his gaze made me shy.

"Hi," he said. "How long have you been back?

"Not long," I said, evasively. I didn't want to admit that I had driven past his place several times since I came back, hoping for a glimpse of him.

“Are you still married?” he asked.

“No,” I replied. “You?”

“No,” he said. “Do you want to be?”

I laughed. “Is that a proposal?”

“Maybe,” he said.

“Do you think maybe we should have coffee first?”

“Good idea. Come to my place and I will make you coffee and show you what I have built on your land.”

He tucked my hand under his arm and took my shopping bag. Our conversation had been light-hearted but there was a depth of communication within it that made my heart skip a beat. I decided to be honest.

“I have been past once or twice.”

He looked at me intently.

“Okay, a few times.”

“But you didn’t write, you didn’t call….”

“Well, you know…” I shrugged. I didn’t know what to say.

Andy asked me about my travels and I told him what I had been doing. We walked happily together towards his home. When we went in, I was delighted with its design and beauty.

“Have a look around while I make coffee.” said Andy.

I walked around the living room and came to a wall with several framed photos. They were shots of the demolition of my house and there was one of me with tears in my eyes. There was another of the new house being constructed. There was a photo of a dandelion.

I walked through the house, admiring everything. Andy caught up with me while I was looking out the bedroom window. Suddenly it felt weird, almost thrilling, to be in a bedroom with him and I think he felt the same way. He turned back to the kitchen and I followed him.

I sat at the kitchen bench while he poured the coffee. He took a seat beside me.

"Do you know when I first saw you?" he asked.

"No."

"I was looking at the properties in the window of an estate agent when you walked by. I saw you and you took my breath away. I followed you in and listened to you telling the agent that you wanted to sell a house that had to be pulled down."

"Is that why you bought it?"

"Yes."

"Oh." I didn't know what to say.

"Would you like to have dinner with me?" he asked.

"Yes," I replied. "When?"

"Tonight?"

"Sure."

"I will pick you up at seven." Andy reached for a pen and paper.

"Oh no, wait. I can't." I whispered. "I just can't."

Andy looked startled and anxious. I looked away. I paused.

"I can't wait that long. I will pick you up at six. I know where you live."

I looked at Andy just in time to see a sweet mixture of relief and forgiveness.

"Don't scare me like that. I have only just found you again."

"Why didn't you say anything to me at the time?" I asked.

"Because you were about to embark on a wonderful adventure. You had just left your home and husband. You needed space and I wanted to give you that space. I told myself that if I was a good boy this year, then maybe I would get what I want next year."

"Have you been married before?"

"No."

"Why not?"

"Because I hadn't met you yet."

"Good line."

"I thought so. It also happens to be true."

I could hardly breathe. It was happening so fast and yet it felt so right. I had to leave.

"I had better go. See you tonight."

Andy saw me to the door and watched me walk down the path to the street.

"Hey!" he called.

I turned and we walked towards each other.

He took my face in his hands and kissed me gently.

“Welcome home.” he said.

I smiled.

Epilogue

Hello again, dear Reader, Anne Holmes taught me to go on rampages of appreciation. I thought you might like to read one. When I think of what I love, another thought follows it. As I write this, the thoughts are flowing faster than I can write. Here is what I appreciate today:

I love knowing I still love Mike. I love knowing that I love me more.

I love knowing that we had thirty great years together.

I love knowing we have two happy, healthy children.

I love knowing I have happy memories that I can draw on whenever I want. I love knowing I had the courage to leave him.

I love remembering the joy, the friendship and the challenges of our years together.

I love believing we will be able to meet one day as friends at family events.

I love knowing that I am strong enough now to do what I want.

I love being able to have worked with AH.

I love knowing that it's getting better every day.

I love the new freedom I have to choose a different life.

I love feeling daring and adventurous.

I love my to-do list, which is made up of things I really want to do.

I love lifting my arms in a cool breeze and watching sunshine on the sea.

I love being able to choose my own happiness.

I love knowing I am the creator of my own reality.

I love knowing that my childcare book will be helpful to carers and children worldwide.

I love this new version of me.

I love knowing I have infinite possibilities.

I love feeling light hearted and invincible. I love having fun.

I love knowing I can make it up as I go along.

I love feeling sure about my next step because it is the next logical step.

I love having clarity, abundance, eagerness, passion, purpose, love, decisiveness and appreciation.

I love being adventurous, determined, excited, daring, exhilarated, expansive, delighted, joyful and free.

I love knowing that life is a group effort and that each one of us has a physical and non-physical cheer squad urging us to go on and do one better than was done before.

And lastly….

I love my wonderful Andy and I love, love, love my life.

THE END

Acknowledgements

This book pays homage to Esther Hicks, from whom
love, humor, kindness and wisdom shine.

Without Esther and (the late) Jerry Hicks and Abraham, this book would not exist. I am very grateful to them for the work they do. I have incorporated many of their strategies with great success into my work as a psychologist, particularly the upstream/downstream metaphor, and I feel honored to be able to use their ideas in this book. I have used phrases from their work, such as 'life is supposed to be fun'; 'get happy'; 'rampage of appreciation'; 'beliefs are just thoughts you keep thinking', 'tuned in, tapped in and turned on'; 'there is no happy ending to an unhappy journey'; 'you can be, do and have whatever you want'; and 'perfection equals endedness'.

For those of you who are familiar with the work of Jerry and Esther Hicks, I hope you enjoy my use of their terms and that you smile when you read a familiar and much-loved concept. While I have conveyed my understanding of 'The Teachings of Abraham', I do not claim to have them down perfectly. For those who understand, I have written the book I wanted to write. For more information regarding many of the ideas presented by the Anne Holmes character in this book, please go to www.abraham-hicks. com or read their book 'Ask and It is Given'.

For those not familiar with Abraham-Hicks, I hope you find this a gentle and unobtrusive introduction to the concept of the law of attraction and the power of thought. I hope that you simply enjoy this book.

I would also like to thank the sages of our time: Richard Bach, Edgar Cayce, Wayne Dyer, Louise L. Hay, Jane Roberts, Tony Robbins, Neale Donald Walsch and Marianne Williamson, who have inspired me to follow my bliss. Many thanks also go to Mike Dooley who lifts my spirits every day.

I would like to thank Lynn Williams for her many good ideas and her encouragement and the real Ryan Galbraith for his patient help with all things technological. I would like to thank Ian Symonds, Solicitor, for his wise legal counsel. Many thanks to Kahren Richardson for her wealth of ideas and beautiful cover design. Special thanks go to Wendy Morriss who assisted with the editing. Her input was invaluable.

I would like also to thank my strong, independent mother Turid Guilford, whose true brain tumor story is told in this book. Thank you to all my good friends named Sue. The character Sue was named in your honor and you know who you are.

Much love to you all,

Terry Guilford

Printed in the United States
By Bookmasters